W9-CFX-949

The Rosh Yeshiva

The Story of Rav Chaim Shmulevitz
the "Stutchiner"

The Rosh Yeshiva

The Story of Rav Chaim Shmulevitz the "Stutchiner"

by
Rav Reuven Grossman

Rendered into English
by Rav Yaakov M. Rapoport

Targum /Feldheim

First published 1988

Hardcover: ISBN 0-944070-03-5
Softcover: ISBN 0-944070-05-1

Phototypeset at Targum Press

Photography: Shaul Morgenstern

Published by:
Targum Press Inc.
22700 W. Eleven Mile Rd.
Southfield, Mich. 48034

Distributed by:
Philipp Feldheim Inc.
200 Airport Executive Park
Spring Valley, N.Y. 10977

Distributed in Israel by:
Nof Books Ltd.
POB 23646
Jerusalem 91235

Printed in Israel

It had been our intention to introduce this work with an essay on the life and works of the author, the late Rav Reuven Grossman, zt"l. When we attempted to prepare such an essay, it became clear to us that only Rav Grossman himself had the ability and skills to portray the greatness and richness of his tragically short, yet full and productive life. It remains for us, therefore, to dedicate this English language rendering of Mo'ach V'Lev *to the memory of HaRav Reuven Ben Menachem Grossman zt"l.*

Targum Press
Southfield, Michigan
Nissan, 5748

CONTENTS

TRANSLATOR'S PREFACE

Mo'ach VeLev, by the late Rav Reuven Grossman, zt"l, the original Hebrew edition of this work, was initially published by Moriah Publishers in 1980 as part of the *Sefer HaZikaron* in memory of HaGaon Rav Chaim Shmulevitz. It has since been published a number of times as an independent work by the authors' widow, Rebbetzin Sheindel Grossman.

Mo'ach VeLev, which was a 'best-seller' in the Hebrew language, has quickly come to be accepted as a classic among biographies of *gedolei Yisroel*.

It is impossible to describe the problems and difficulties involved in translating the original Hebrew edition into English. The author's superb literary-rabbinic style, which gives *Mo'ach VeLev* its special flavor, and the very essence of the work—the life of HaGaon Rav Chaim Shmulevitz through his own words, principally through his *shmuessen*—made a faithful translation a most formidable task.

This task would have been insurmountable without the cooperation of Reb Tuvia Krevit, who spent long months with the translator painstakingly checking the original draft of the manuscript and superbly editing it for the English reading public, and without the consistent advice and help of Rav Moshe Dombey, the editorial assistance of Mr. David Green, and the meticulous copy editing and proofreading of Mrs. Ita Oleskar.

Special mention has to be made of the warm encouragement Rebbetzin Sheindel Grossman gave to help ensure that the English edition would be a true translation of the original Hebrew and the efforts of Dr. Eliezer Ebner of Jerusalem in furthering this aim. Reb Yaacov Feldheim of Feldheim Publishers, Jerusalem, is also to be thanked for his valuable editorial comments which helped bring the book to its final form.

The translator humbly offers *shevach vehodaya* to the *Ribono Shel Olam* for the *zechus* of bringing this work to the English reading public and hopes and prays that the tremendous *chizuk* that he and all those involved in the preparation of this work received from its contents be shared by all who read it.

Yaakov Mordechai Rapoport
Adar 5748
Jerusalem

AUTHOR'S FOREWORD
TO THE HEBREW EDITION

There are many similarities between a painter and a writer. One works with his brush, the other with his pen. One sketches with the richness of his colors, the other with the richness of his language. Each attempts to portray an image of his model, one through the eyes of the flesh and the other through the eyes of the spirit.

How can the painter hope to encompass all the details of the image he is painting—to distinguish each hair, reveal every pore, describe width, length, and depth, and also discriminate among a multitude of shades? And how can the writer hope to climb to the heights of the spirit, to observe the vista of the infinite, or to descend into the depths of the soul, to analyze its profound niches and communicate an understanding of its treasures?

Neither the painter nor the writer can expect to portray an image in a manner that exceeds his ability and sensitivity, or with a talent that surmounts his perception. Rav Chaim was beyond perception, even by those who understood the qualities that define great people. One of the *gedolim* of our

generation characterized Rav Chaim as one who could best be
described as an *acharon*—a description which we have only a
limited ability to understand.

How disappointed will be those who had hoped to find in
this book a full image and characterization of him. Even his
relatives, intimate friends, and closest *talmidim* are unable to
describe from their firsthand knowledge such an image.

Rav Chaim explained the vast gap between the external
and the internal, between the revealed actions of man and the
driving force behind them, which is the essence of humanity:

> It is not the action that expresses the greatness of an
> individual, rather, the greatness of an individual lends
> substance to the action.
>
> Because Yehudah admitted his misconduct with
> Tamar, he merited that the tribes appoint him to rule
> over them. Nevertheless, that admission was not
> enough to make him deserving the World to Come.
> In human eyes, that action meant royalty—but up
> there...?
>
> "The Angel of Death could not gain access to Rav
> Chiya, so one day, he adopted the guise of a poor man
> and came and tapped at Rav Chiya's gate. He said,
> 'Bring me some bread.' Some bread was brought to him.
> He then said to Rav Chiya, 'Don't you treat the poor
> kindly, sir? Why don't you befriend me, a poor man,
> and give me bread with your own hand?' Rav Chiya
> opened the door to him, whereupon the Angel of Death,
> revealing a fiery rod, made him yield his soul" [*Moed
> Katan* 28a]. Through human eyes, we see Rav Chiya's
> action as an act of charity. The Angel of Death saw the
> greatness of the man that lay behind the action, and
> appreciated that, more than just giving away his bread,
> Rav Chiya was giving away his whole soul.

On the other hand, we see a charitable person, but it's possible that his actions are insufficient due to the greatness of his soul. There are charitable people whose actions appear tremendous; but if they are not doing all they can do, their great acts contain a deficiency, their virtue a humiliation.

This book is not a biography, a hagiography, or a composite picture of Rav Chaim Shmulevitz. At most, it is a random collection of assorted points which have been put down on paper. Only the reader's ability to tap into the upper limits of his perception and fill in missing gaps will enable him to touch the edge of the great personality of Rav Chaim Shmulevitz.

All we can hope to do is to note the details as they were told to us and record them faithfully, accurately, and clearly, while attempting to keep some semblance of flow. All this is done with the clear knowledge that each story, thought, and idea could be elaborated and linked through any number of connections, each different in its essence, each elevating the entire picture to a level of greater spiritual significance.

From all the thousands of details, small and large, that were available to make up this book, we took only those stories and reflections which had reliable sources. Where we were in doubt about a situation, even about an anecdote that has somehow become well known, we indicated that it is only rumored.

Our publication schedule allowed us only three months from beginning to end if we were to bring out this book by the first *yahrzeit* of Rav Chaim. This limited our interviews to tens among the thousands who knew him. Only a few sparks of memory were rescued from oblivion as we vicariously relived the unforgettable experiences of those privileged to have had personal contact with him.

We listened with great attentiveness, even to those who, after tens of years of intimate familiarity, could recount nothing besides the fact that Rav Chaim was always animated in his learning. And we were deeply impressed by those who, with a holy reverence, shook their heads and said, "Take your shoes off your feet. The place where you are standing is where he stood—it is holy." We are indebted to all of them.

We did not seek sensationalism or look for glitter. The search was for the daily events of his life, his reality, to be presented in a meaningful manner and factually consistent—in short, the man.

Among those who reminisced for us were *roshei yeshiva, mashgichim, talmidei chachomim, baalei mussar, talmidim,* and loved ones. There were those who wished to remain anonymous, and we made no distinctions. Except for a few people who are no longer alive, we have not mentioned any of the names of those who confided in us. We did not intend in any way to minimize the great contributions of the people we interviewed. But this is not a history book. It is a book about one individual. All the events and bits and pieces are intended solely to yield some small idea of the amazing saga which was the life of Rav Chaim Shmulevitz.

Reuven Grossman

Although extreme saintliness is a "luxury" not granted to everyone (those who do not possess it are not punished), those whose ancestors were famous for extreme saintliness in any respect have the ability to attain it as if it were normally attainable. If they do not, they deserve to be punished.

(*Me'iri*, *Shabbos*, 51a)

The heights of a father's spiritual attainment must constitute the foundation of his son's behavior. A son who neglects this deserves to be punished.

(Rav Chaim Shmulevitz)

ONE

THE FOUNDATION

T HE GAON AND TZADDIK Rav Refoel Alter Shmulevitz was still a young man when he served as *rosh yeshiva* in the town of Stutchin in Poland. Those who knew him there cannot forget his warm and shining personality, which stood out even among those giants who were his contemporaries, the great *roshei yeshiva* of Poland and Lithuania. His attainment at such a young age of a respected position in the ranks of the Lithuanian *gaonim* was due to his extraordinary genius and righteousness, which still evoke trembling in all those who knew him. He was a *godol*, proficient in all areas of Torah, *mussar*, and kabbalah. One day, his son Chaim asked him if he understood the kabbalistic work he was studying. Rav Alter replied, "Like *Chumash* and *Rashi.*"

There were no limits to Rav Alter's *ahavas haTorah* or sense of responsibility. He taught and also bore the entire burden of running the Stutchin Yeshiva while he himself lived in extreme poverty. At the same time, he fashioned the raw qualities and talents of his students with a craftsman's hand.

On one occasion, at the beginning of a school year, the boys of a town who were to be sent to study in *yeshivos* were divided into two groups. The brighter ones were sent to the famous Slabodka Yeshiva, the others to Stutchin. At the end of the year, it was apparent that those who had been sent to Stutchin to study under the watchful eye of Rav Alter and benefit from his total dedication to his students had far surpassed their friends in Slabodka.

Rebbetzin Ettel, the daughter of the Alter of Novaradok, was a perfect complement to Rav Alter. She was a *tzaddekes* of rare, noble character and unique benevolence. Into their home, which was permeated with Torah and *chessed*, a son was born on the second day of Rosh Hashanah 5662 (1901). He was named Chaim Leib, in memory of the Gaon Rav Chaim Leib Stavisker. He was to illuminate the Torah world for sixty years.

*   *   *

Graduates of the Stutchin Yeshiva and other Jews who passed through Stutchin in Rav Chaim's childhood years recall him as the *masmid* of the yeshiva. Day and night he sat and toiled in Torah study with his father, from whom he acquired the foundation of his approach to learning. Until his dying day, he considered his father to be his rebbe.

During the First World War, Rav Alter fled to Grodno, where he founded a yeshiva that would one day become world famous. He returned to Stutchin some years later and was succeeded in Grodno by the Gaon Rav Shimon Shkop.

Young Chaim was orphaned at the age of sixteen. His father and mother passed away within six months of each other in 1918. Before his death, Rav Alter called his son to him and entreated him to assume responsibility for his two young sisters and baby brother. The tragedy of his parents' death left young Chaim with the sole duty of providing for the orphaned family's material needs. His sense of responsibility—the trait which he was later to espouse as the essence of humanity—demanded that he find a source of income. During the great famine that swept through Poland after the war, he spent his working hours in the marketplace, eking out the pitiful sum necessary for bare survival. The rest of the day and night he spent immersed in Torah study. His sisters and brother cannot recall ever seeing him sleep in those difficult times. He spent long nights writing *chiddushei Torah* that he had developed during the hectic hours of toil in the marketplace.

From early childhood, Rav Chaim trained himself to analyze and meditate on the events he witnessed. Such events, which he often discussed in later years, gave rise to lessons in how to live morally. When presenting his students with his detailed analyses of parent-child relationships, which contained key concepts based on *Chazal*, he typically illustrated each concept with a reminiscence of his childhood days in Stutchin. Even the Stutchin marketplace served as a school for Rav Chaim. He illustrated a fundamental concept in human relationships with a story about market day.

> The Rosh writes, "Do not interfere in an argument that does not concern you because the two parties will eventually make peace between themselves" [*Orchos Chaim*, chap. 65].
>
> Avshalom wanted to cause a rift among the people. He knew they would not wish to interfere in a quarrel between him and his father, Dovid HaMelech. Everyone knows the Rosh's rule. He, therefore, turned to Achitophel for advice.

How does the *posuk* describe Achitophel's advice? "And the advice of Achitophel in those days was like that inquired from the oracle of God" [*Shmuel* 2, 16:23]. Advice on how to involve other people in a quarrel with Dovid HaMelech can be described as advice which could only be received from an oracle of God.

"And Achitophel advised Avshalom, 'Come to your father's concubines...'" [*Shmuel* 2, 16:21]. This would be an unforgivable act. The principle, "Eventually the two parties will make peace," would not apply....

Concerning this advice the prophet said, "The advice of Achitophel, which he gave in those days, was like that of a man who inquired from the oracle of God." Without this advice...the people would ask themselves, "Who asked you to interfere?"

Practical experience also teaches us the Rosh's rule. I remember market day in Stutchin. Thousands of people used to come from nearby villages and towns. The market was a major source of income for the traders and villagers. When the time came for everyone to go home, the place would be strewn with bodies of the injured, their arms broken, their legs broken, their faces smashed. Why were so many injured? It is only natural that on market day not everyone sees eye-to-eye...a glass of brandy is also a good reason to fight....Two people would get into a fight, and a third person would come along and try to calm them down. The adversaries would immediately join forces, turn against their "benefactor," saying, "Who asked you to interfere?" and beat him to death....In the end, they would slap each other on the back and make peace, exactly as the Rosh proclaims. These incidents occurred all the time....

"Interfering in an argument that does not concern you." Ninety percent of the issues we involve ourselves with are arguments and quarrels that in reality do not concern us....

Reminiscences and childhood memories, pondered and analyzed by Rav Chaim, became an integral part of his world view. Nothing escaped his discerning eye. Everyday events passed through the testing ground of a brilliant mind and sensitive soul to be processed and refined until they became pure ethical doctrines.

*   *   *

God was with the boy. The boy grew up and lived in the desert where he became an expert archer.

(Bereshis 21:26)

What does the phrase "God was with the boy" mean? I don't know. But the Torah clearly tells us that God helped him without limit. What was the result of this tremendous help from God? An expert archer! How can this be understood? It is simple: God's help is comparable to rain. Whatever man sows, the rain helps to grow.

(Rav Chaim Shmulevitz)

His revered father's *petirah* left Rav Chaim without a rebbe. Growing up in his father's house, however, had clearly shaped him; he carried within him extensive teachings and spiritual wealth, all stamped with the imprint of his upbringing. In addition to methodology and breadth in Torah learning, he had absorbed the spiritual greatness of his parents' home in its years of glory. Responsibility and self-sacrifice, extraordinary acts of *tzedakah* and *chessed*, and unlimited *ahavas*

haTorah, these and their practical expressions came together
in a personality which hungered for spiritual improvement, in
spite of its already great spiritual standing and, indeed, perhaps because of it.

Rav Chaim told the story of the visit of the renowned
mashgiach of the Mir Yeshiva, the Gaon and Tzaddik Rav
Yeruchem Levovitz, to Stutchin. It was before Rav Yeruchem
had assumed his position at the Mir, and Rav Alter asked him
to remain in Stutchin and become the *mashgiach* of the yeshiva
there:

> Rav Alter told Rav Yeruchem, "I have no financial
> incentives to offer you, but I am prepared to give to you
> my one and only shirt, which I am wearing"!
>
> Do you really think that it was so necessary to
> employ Rav Yeruchem as *mashgiach*? At that time the
> Rabbi of Stutchin was the Gaon and Tzaddik Rav Leib
> Chasman, one of the great *baalei mussar* of the gene-
> ration. Do you really think that he did not fill the
> *mussar* requirements of the yeshiva?
>
> The lesson is obvious! A person should be prepared
> to sacrifice his only shirt for even the smallest increase
> of *mussar*.

Rav Chaim kept the memory of his father alive with words of
deep admiration and respect. Whenever he cited one of his
father's novel interpretations or told a story about him, he
would emphasize that he was fulfilling the mitzvah of *kibbud
av*. Thus he taught a practical and striking lesson in this
mitzvah, which he defined in a unique fashion.

> When a person honors his father *despite* what his father
> is, he has not fulfilled the mitzvah. A person must honor

his father *because* of what he is! A son has to rack his
brains to achieve maximum awareness of his father's
greatness in order to discover his father's uniqueness
and honor him accordingly. A person who is unable to
find a unique dimension in his father does not fulfill
the mitzvah.

Rav Chaim would relate how Rav Alter worked tirelessly to
systematize his thoughts in order to reach maximum awareness of his own father's greatness. Rav Alter maintained that
in spite of the fact that his father was a simple *melamed* in a
cheder, the effort he expended in educating his students was
unique.

*   *   *

Rav Alter's early *petirah* ended a life of intense *avodas
Hashem* and acquisition of Torah knowledge. He left a large
store of writings and amazing *chiddushei Torah* on many
subjects. Rav Chaim diligently rewrote and edited them, and
carried the manuscripts with him on all his journeys and
wanderings. He protected them as the apple of his eye. When
some manuscripts were confiscated at a customs checkpoint in
Soviet Russia, he refused to be comforted. Until his dying day,
he was unable to forget their loss or even come to terms with
it. On one occasion, Rav Chaim wished to send the manuscripts abroad for safety. He gave them to an emissary with
detailed instructions on how to carry them, care for them, and
avoid mislaying them. "These are my whole life!" he proclaimed, waving the manuscripts in the air.

After his father's death, Rav Chaim remained in Stutchin
for two and a half years. In addition to shouldering sole
responsibility for his family's material welfare, he struggled to

ensure its spiritual survival. One hour of learning followed another, night followed night, *chavrusa* followed *chavrusa*, *chiddush* followed *chiddush*. With endless effort, with a love that bitter reality could not extinguish, with inexplicable and uncompromising effort, the young boy remained totally devoted to Torah study. (Those days of material and spiritual gloom, saturated with difficulty and hardship, would later be described by Rav Chaim with the words of the *Yalkut* on *Koheles*: " 'Also my wisdom stood me in good stead' (*Koheles* 2:9). The Torah that I studied in [God's] anger [in time of extreme hardship] remained with me." [*Af*, the word for "also" in Hebrew, also means "anger."])

And then, in the depths of despair, he suddenly received a call from the Gaon Rav Shimon Shkop to take a position as *maggid shiur* in the Grodno Yeshiva. The young genius arrived in Grodno in the summer of 1921. He was nineteen years old. His knowledge of Torah encompassed the entire Talmud with all the *poskim*, *rishonim*, and *acharonim*. In addition, he carried a heavy load of life experience.

When Rav Shimon Shkop was asked why he selected the young boy from Stutchin as *maggid shiur* over other possible candidates, he quickly answered, "It is true that there are other suitable candidates to say a *shiur*, but no one can instill love of Torah into his students as Rav Chaim 'Stutchiner' can!" On another occasion, after *farhering* Rav Chaim's students, he said to them, "One thing I can tell you about your rebbe, when I was his age, I didn't come up to his ankles in Torah knowledge."

The department dealing with the younger students in the Grodno Yeshiva was an autonomous *yeshiva ketana* with three class levels. The new *maggid shiur's* students were chosen from the ranks of older boys who had already graduated the junior yeshiva. Rav Chaim's *shiurim* were dazzling. His clear presentation of the most complicated and profound talmudic subjects was extremely popular, and his audience increased from day to day. His whole being was enveloped in a refreshing vitality derived from the very essence of his existence— Torah! After a *shiur,* it was not unusual to see him run between the benches of the *beis hamedrash,* gather together his students, and shout, "Hurry! You must listen! I have found a new way of explaining the *Yerushalmi!"* Often, those who were ready to graduate refused to leave the *shiur* and make room for new students. Long after graduation they could still be found hiding in the women's gallery listening secretly to their beloved *maggid shiur's shiurim.*

Rav Chaim absorbed much of Rav Shimon's unique *derech halimud,* and many of his *yesodos* were based on the *gaon's* analytical approach to Talmud. He transcribed Rav Shimon's *shiurim,* and for many years, his notebooks provided the only available written source for them. After Rav Shimon published his major work, *Shaarei Yosher,* Rav Chaim's notes were still used to clarify difficult points in it. Rav Chaim's transcripts of these *shiurim* added a special dimension and sharpness to *Shaarei Yosher.* The young *maggid shiur* would review these transcripts many times in depth before repeating them to students. When he did so, they had a totally new flavor.

Part of his greatness lay in his capacity to examine a single point from all angles and perspectives, even when it appeared to be simple and clear-cut. In order to remember just one minor detail, he would review again and again. A former *talmid* recalls bringing a question to Rav Chaim. As he approached him, the *talmid* saw that he was totally immersed in a *Rambam.* He did not notice the *talmid,* who decided to count the number of times Rav Chaim repeated the Rambam's words. Although he had no way of knowing how many repetitions had already occurred, he watched Rav Chaim repeat them twenty-five times before he was noticed. It was an experience the *talmid* would never forget.

Rav Chaim's obstinate, penetrating, insatiable studiousness was a learning vehicle that made an indelible impression on his *talmidim*. Standard conceptions of diligence paled in the face of the extraordinary effort Rav Chaim invested in his studies. Those who were privileged to be close to him acquired completely new criteria by which to measure everything relating to Torah study.

Rav Chaim continued to study with a *chavrusa* with great diligence as he had done since childhood. After a long night of studying *Yerushalmi* with his *chavrusa,* he would review on the way back to their rooms to catch a short nap. Every landmark on the way became a station to pause at and review—the last row of benches, the door, the gate to the courtyard—and at every station, they would stop and review again. They would pass an electric pole on the long village road to their lodgings. With the fine humor that typified him, Rav Chaim once stopped at the pole and exclaimed with a smile, "An excellent place to review once again." These endless reviews were usually terminated close to the time of *shacharis.* *Talmid* and rebbe often had to return directly to the *beis hamedrash* to be on time for davening. The late night learning was carried on in an unassuming manner; from a comment the *mashgiach* made, it was apparent that he knew nothing about it. They completed the entire *Talmud Yerushalmi* in less than six months in sessions which lasted six to eight hours.

In Grodno, Rav Chaim was conscripted into the army. It took him some months to obtain a discharge. On Sundays, when some soldiers were given short leave and others remained in the camp to carry out different tasks, Rav Chaim would disappear into a deserted part of the army base where his students had secreted themselves in some bushes to listen to his *shiur.*

He was accustomed to write to his family in Stutchin every week. If a week passed without a reply, he would hurry from Grodno to Stutchin to see if, God forbid, anything had happened.

In the month of Elul, Rav Chaim would travel to the Novaradok Yeshiva in Bialystock (which was headed by his uncle) to, as he put it, "warm up spiritually." Many years later, he recalled these visits with yearning and described the "very special flavor of studying Torah in penury" which one experienced in Novaradok.

Rav Chaim was a *maggid shiur* in Grodno Yeshiva for about four years. By 1925, when he was twenty-four years old, he had become famous throughout the country. The name of the *masmid* of Stutchin was renowned among the students of Polish and Lithuanian *yeshivos*. The nickname Rav Chaim "Stutchiner," which recalled his extraordinary roots, stayed with him his whole life. Even chassidic students from Poland would talk about the "special personality from Stutchin."

When a number of his friends transferred to the Mir, he decided to join them, but he did not just pick himself up and leave Grodno for Mir. He took leave of his beloved students, his rebbe, Rav Shimon, and his position in Grodno, and "carried himself into exile." He spent a short time in the Mir Yeshiva in 1925, then went into seclusion in a small township called Antopola, where he diligently studied with a *chavrusa* for six months. Emissaries were sent by the *rosh yeshiva* of the Mir, the Gaon Rav Eliezer Yehudah Finkel, and its *mashgiach*, the Tzaddik Rav Yeruchem Levovitz, requesting that he rejoin the yeshiva. Rav Chaim returned to Mir permanently; from this time on, he would never leave the Mir Yeshiva. When he returned, some of his students from Grodno were already anxiously awaiting him. They could not bear to be parted from their beloved rebbe.

The words of the Torah are sparse in one place and plentiful in another.

(Yerushalmi, Rosh Hashanah 3:5)

What one verse leaves unsaid the other elaborates.

(Midrash Tanchuma, Chukas 23)

Nu, is it then possible to manage without knowing the entire Torah?

(Rav Chaim Shmulevitz)

TWO

TOIL IN THE TORAH

Y OUNG CHAIM arrived at the Mir Yeshiva as Rav Chaim
"Stutchiner." The very name was legendary, recalling a
yeshiva student's meteoric rise in the world of Torah
scholars. In the atmosphere that pervaded most of the Lithuanian *yeshivos* of the time, the main criteria for evaluating a
student's worth were his level of Torah knowledge and powers
of logical analysis. Rav Chaim's reputation preceded his arrival
in Mir, and his acquaintances who were already there attested
to his outstanding credentials in these areas. From the start,
stories of his amazing diligence and astounding breadth of
knowledge gave him an exalted standing in the eyes of the
student body. Despite the fact that Mir students and faculty
were the elite of the Torah world, Rav Chaim is clearly
remembered by everyone as a cut above all his contemporaries.

If Rav Chaim's erudition had been considered exceptional
on his arrival at Grodno Yeshiva, one can imagine the impact
it made by the time he arrived at the Mir. He could repeat
verbatim entire sections and chapters of the *Shulchan Aruch*

with all the commentaries. The complete range of later-day halachic and talmudic literature, the staple of Lithuanian yeshiva students, was also at his fingertips. One student recounts how they were learning the *Nesivos* when Rav Chaim suddenly stopped and exclaimed, "There are some words missing here!" Although the text was completely understandable as it was—the language flowed smoothly—Rav Chaim insisted that some of the text was missing. After an examination of a number of different editions of the *Nesivos*, he was proven correct.

In talmudic discussion, he would often refer to obscure midrashic collections, the names of which are not commonly known. It was rumored that he was familiar with the contents of every *sefer* in the Grodno Yeshiva library down to the smallest details and that he could quote from each one of them word for word. It did not take long for another rumor to circulate—Rav Chaim had added the Mir Yeshiva library to his list of conquests!

Amazingly enough, he still spent the best part of the day studying with a *chavrusa*, which left him only a few hours to himself. When did he find the time to acquire his wealth of knowledge in subjects he did not study with a *chavrusa?* This question has never been answered. Somehow, he managed it, and by doing so, he seemed to prove that there is time for everything. No new *sefer* in the yeshiva library left his hands until he had studied it in its entirety. The time he found for these in-depth perusals was that brief period that is neither day nor night.

Rav Chaim's greatness in Torah and the esteem in which he was held in no way influenced the choice of *seforim* he studied. Any *sefer* that came his way received his undivided, maximum attention, as if it had been written by one of the world's greatest Torah authorities. Only after patient and exhaustive deliberation and concentration would he pass judgment. On one occasion, Rav Chaim explained how he could disregard the greatness, or lack of greatness, of a particular *sefer* and its author:

> The Gemara [*Sanhedrin* 7a] relates there was a man who used to say, "When love between my wife and myself was strong, we could have made our bed on a sword blade. Now that our love has grown weak, a bed of sixty cubits is not enough for us."
>
> "There was a man who used to say..." The Gemara doesn't even bother to mention his name—an anonymous person. But see what Mr. Anonymous knew! He made a statement, and for us his statement is Torah!

Any new idea or approach that Rav Chaim found in a *sefer* was immediately incorporated into his Torah knowledge. In later years, he did not always remember the sources for some ideas and approaches, but he was always particular to point out that they were not original. His introduction to a talmudic topic began, "On this topic there are sixteen (eighteen, fourteen, twenty...) sources that have to be considered and analyzed." Then he would list all the sources. "Here...there... there...that *sefer*...this journal...that essay..." He would cite all the sources he knew, and it was rare for his students to discover additional sources. His delivery gave the impression that he was reading from a prepared subject index. Rav Chaim had such "indexes" for the entire Torah.

His thoughts were arranged in a completely orderly fashion. He would not only cite titles and authors of *seforim,* but numbers, chapters, sections, and subsections. At times, it was obvious that some questions—particularly from younger students—were only attempts to test his total recall. Rav Chaim's *chavrusos* pointed this out to him, and he retorted, "You are right, but at least they gain an idea of how much one has to study." Although his encyclopedic knowledge made a great impression, the profound and subtle connections he established proved that it was far more than a well-ordered collection of facts, neatly arranged and edited.

Even the most advanced students felt like children when they measured themselves against Rav Chaim. In his shadow, they concretely perceived the "infinity of Torah knowledge."

In his student days, one of today's great Torah scholars wrote a *sefer* of *chiddushim* and presented the manuscript to Rav Chaim for his criticism. The author was then sure that all his *chiddushim* were original because Rav Chaim did not inform him that any of them were to be found in other published works. (In fact, one *chiddush* in this *sefer* does appear in the *Ohr Some'ach*, but graduates of the Mir explain that the yeshiva library did not purchase the *Ohr Some'ach* until a much later date.) When the manuscript was finally published, Rav Chaim was seen to study it at length with great enthusiasm. One student whispered to the author, "Now Rav Chaim knows your book better than you do."

Another contemporary authority relates that he wrote his *chiddushim* while Rav Chaim was still in Grodno, but delayed publication until Rav Chaim could examine them. When he visited the yeshiva in which the author was studying, Rav Chaim read the manuscript from beginning to end and commented, "One third of it contains *yeshivishe Torah*, one third contains *chiddushim* found in other works, and one third is original." The author only published those *chiddushim* that fell into the third category.

When the American committee of the Mir and the yeshiva executive decided to award monetary prizes to *talmidim* who successfully passed an examination on the memorization of five hundred *blatt Gemara*, it was obvious that Chaim "Stutchiner" would not be allowed to enter the contest. The Gaon Rav Yitzchak Safsal, whose own *bekius* was considered phenomenal, once remarked, "There are three *beki'im* in this generation: Rav Chaim Ozer Grodzenski, Rav Chaim "Stutchiner," and myself."

Rav Chaim once traveled to Vilna to visit the great Torah sage of that generation, Rav Chaim Ozer Grodzenski. Although Rav Chaim Ozer was sitting and talking with a prominent rabbi, when Rav Chaim entered the room, he stood up. The rabbi asked him why he had stood up for an unknown young student. Rav Chaim Ozer answered, "When the Mir Yeshiva library walks in, I stand up."

* * *

Rav Pereda had a student to whom he taught every lesson four hundred times before he could master it.

(Eruvin 54b)

Chazal *praise Rav Pereda. I will tell you the truth. I am impressed with the student for wanting to hear a* shiur *four hundred times—such a love of Torah!*

(Rav Chaim Shmulevitz)

It was common for Rav Chaim to eat a piece of bread and some herring for breakfast, then study enthusiastically for thirty hours or more without a break. He would then snatch a nap and return to his exhausting schedule. Sometimes he would be found fast asleep under his bench, having collapsed from sheer exhaustion. Even when eating, his mind was still active. He had great difficulty davening with concentration because his mind was constantly at work, asking, answering, comparing, and rejecting. As long as he could keep his eyes open there was no distinction between day and night, and, in fact, the later at night it was, the clearer his mind and the greater his concentration. The big mystery was, when and for how long did he sleep? For years on end, he studied with *chavrusos* until well after midnight and started learning with other *chavrusos* at three in the morning. A young student who once asked Rav Chaim to learn with him before davening received the reply, "Sure. Will one in the morning be convenient for you?"

Late one night he had finished learning with a *chavrusa* and was on his way out of the *beis hamedrash* when he absentmindedly picked up a *Shaar HaMelech* which was lying on the table and started reading it. He was discovered in the morning, standing in the same spot, still totally absorbed in the *Shaar HaMelech*.

Expressions like, "I know," or "I have already learned this," were not a part of his lexicon. Rav Chaim derided those who surrendered to feelings of self-satisfaction in their studies or tried to give the impression that they had mastered a particular topic. "The *Chumash* is the same *Chumash*," he would argue, "but how many times have we reviewed it?"

Citing the Gemara he often expressed the opinion that review is new study.

"Why are the words of Torah compared to a fig tree? Just as a fig tree's fruits do not all ripen at the same time—whenever one searches, he finds more figs—so it is with Torah. The more one studies, the more relish he discovers in it" [*Eruvin* 54a].

The more one studies the very same words of Torah, the more relish he discovers in them, because every review must contain a *chiddush*. If it does not, it is not a review.

The concept of a *chiddush* had a broad and special meaning for Rav Chaim. The same gemara in *Eruvin* continues with the story of Rav Pereda. Rav Chaim commented:

I am puzzled. How do these two gemaras fit together? What *chiddush* could Rav Pereda add the hundredth time he taught the lesson to his student if the student had not grasped the basic principles presented in the first explanation? This is not a question. Every time Rav Pereda taught the lesson, he added a tremendous *chiddush*—additional levels of patience!

Rav Chaim's *ahavas haTorah* did not distinguish between more or less interesting subject matter. Entire *sugyos*, which are often described by *lamdonim* as "dry," would be reviewed by Rav Chaim hundreds of times. He was able to review every subsection of the Shach's commentary on the *Shulchan Aruch* dozens of times without tiring. One student could not contain his amazement at hearing Rav Chaim repeat monotonously to himself a well-known mishnah from a gemara studied in all *yeshivos*. The student volunteered that witnessing this scene was the reason he stopped using his favorite expression, "What more can you really say about this gemara?" Others testify to the many occasions they listened carefully to Rav Chaim repeating a gemara to himself and felt that each time he was understanding that gemara in a different light. Every time he repeated it, from his emphases, which were varied and changing, from his short pauses and long silences, it was clear that he was making endless observations and deductions. To anyone who found himself in his company, the words of the Gemara (*Chagigah* 9b), "He who repeats his chapter a hundred times is not to be compared to he who repeats it a hundred and one times," came to life.

Rav Chaim said that there were topics he had reviewed thousands of times before he was satisfied that he understood them. There were other topics he had reviewed thousands of times without such satisfaction. Many of these occupied him for years. Sometimes the study of a completely different issue would shed light on one of them, and points that seemingly bore no connection would suddenly come together, producing a clear and true understanding. There is no describing his ecstasy when this happened. On one occasion, toward the end of his life, when one such issue suddenly became clear to him—he finally understood a comment of Rav Akiva Eiger that had puzzled and worried him for many years—Rav Chaim exclaimed joyfully, "For fifty years I haven't slept because of Rav Akiva Eiger's comment. Only now have I merited to understand it."

Many of his talmudic expositions and *chiddushim* simply proceeded from his wealth of knowledge. Every small detail, even those he understood clearly from their sources, had to fit into the total context of his Torah knowledge and be harmonized with *Shass* and all its commentaries. When explaining his method of study, he always quoted *Chazal*: "All the words of Torah are necessary to one another, for what one verse leaves unsaid the other elaborates."

His encyclopedic knowledge not only elicited numerous contradictions and questions, but also provided the tools to answer them. The constant search to understand the Gemara in the context of the endless details and facts at his command resulted in phenomenal talmudic expositions. Nonetheless, Rav Chaim never viewed his ability to create *chiddushim* as an automatic by-product of his learning. He constantly feared that his students would take this ability for granted and therefore not take his *chiddushim* seriously. Once, he commented to one of his *chavrusos*, "It kills me to create a *chiddush*."

He viewed toil in Torah as an end in itself, and he would often discuss such toil in his *shmuessen*, commenting on the goodness hidden in it and the dangers of refraining from it.

* * *

Parshas Bechukosai does not discuss commandments and transgressions. Our rabbis do not say that "If you follow my laws" means you should be occupied in Torah study, but that "If you follow my laws" means you should toil in Torah study. Thus, it is possible to study Torah without toil.

The Torah continues, "And if you will not listen to Me..." What does this phrase refer to? Not being occupied in the study of Torah? No. Certainly not. *Chazal* interpret the phrase, "And if you will not exert effort in studying Torah..." to mean you *will* be occupied in Torah study without exerting effort. Torah study that does not involve exertion is described as "not listening to Me."

The Torah then describes the blessings that will be heaped on those who "do listen to Me" and the curses that will fall on those who "do not listen to Me." The vast difference between blessings and curses starkly delineates the enormous difference between the *madregos* of Torah study with exertion and Torah study without exertion.

* * *

A student once asked Rav Chaim how to succeed in knowing the entire *Shass*. Shaken, Rav Chaim responded, "You need to *know Shass*?! You need to become ill over *Shass!*" (*Vissen Shass darfst du?! Krenken auf Shass darfst du!*)

It might have seemed to some that Rav Chaim learned Torah with a blind, uncontrollable drive, disregarding time, place, and personal circumstance, his great *ahavas haTorah* simply compelling him to study with vigor and strength until utter exhaustion. In reality, this was not the case. Because Rav Chaim's whole being was saturated with pure *yiras shomayim*, he foresaw situations and carefully planned his actions, calculating time for learning and *chavrusos* to ensure that the flow of *hasmadah* was not broken in any way. An anecdote about one *Tzom Gedalya* during the early years of his studies at the Mir Yeshiva illustrates his careful calculations.

The long hours of davening on Rosh Hashanah did not leave much time for learning. The *masmidim* of the yeshiva tried to learn a little on *motzo'ei* Rosh Hashanah. Knowing it would be difficult to learn on *Tzom Gedalya*, one of the *bochurim* pushed himself to learn through the night following Rosh Hashanah. The next morning after *shacharis*, he retired to his room. He returned to the *beis hamedrash* for *mincha*, thoroughly exhausted from fasting, as he had expected. While learning the previous night, he thought he heard someone learning in another part of the *beis hamedrash*—it was Rav Chaim. Before daybreak Rav Chaim ate, then he davened and went to bed. Later in the morning, he returned to the *beis hamedrash* refreshed and ready to learn as if it were a regular day. A casual comment he made to one of his friends before leaving the *beis hamedrash* revealed his careful planning: "Let *him* learn through the night. *I'm* going to sleep!"

Time and time again, Rav Chaim demonstrated an uncanny ability to predict situations and plan his actions to maximize Torah study. In later years, with a beautiful parable from the Midrash, he cautioned against the clever and cunning manipulations of the *yetzer hora* to prevent Torah study.

The Midrash [*Bereshis Rabbah* 22:66] tells how dogs used to hang around the doorway of a baker's shop in the Roman marketplace. The dogs would pretend they were sleeping while furtively eyeing the well-laden trays of goodies, which exuded appetizing aromas. What does a dog want? One roll! Will the baker allow the dog to steal one roll? Of course not! He carefully protects the rolls from the dogs.

The dogs in the Roman marketplace would pretend they were sleeping and then take advantage of the one split second when the baker turned away to upset a whole tray of goodies. In the ensuing tumult, they would snatch one roll. After the tumult quieted down, the baker would take stock and say to himself, "Not too bad, not too bad. Only one roll lost."

Such is the approach of the *yetzer hora*. He wants us to err in one small detail. This has been taught by *Chazal*. "Such are the wiles of the *yetzer hora*. Today he says to him, 'Do this.' Tomorrow he tells him, 'Do that,' until he bids him go and serve idols" [*Shabbos* 105b]. No sensible-thinking, stable person will allow the *yetzer hora* to foil him and trip him up. But the *Chovas HaLevavos* says, "You sleep, but he is awake" [*Shaar Yichud HaMaaseh*, chap. 5]. The *yetzer hora* has patience. He waits for a moment of inattention, then creates a tumult, putting a person into a sudden, difficult crisis that makes him believe much is about to be lost. When the tumult dies down, the person takes stock and concludes that the *yetzer hora* has only succeeded in tripping him up on one small detail, and he feels good. It's not as terrible a tragedy as he believed it would be. He doesn't realize that this is all the *yetzer hora* wanted.

What *does* the *yetzer hora* want? That a yeshiva *bochur* should cancel one session with a *chavrusa*. What sensible yeshiva *bochur* would listen to him? Not one! What does the *yetzer hora* do? He persuades the yeshiva *bochur* that it is worthwhile to make a *mishmar*—learn through the night, nothing less. The *bochur* is so full of energy and eager to fulfill this plan that he even looks for a *chavrusa*. *Nu!* He learns as usual until midnight, but before beginning his *mishmar*, he has to snatch a nap for an hour or two. He has, after all, spent a tiring day toiling in Torah study....The following morning he learns quite well; however, by midday he feels a bit tired. At lunchtime our *masmid* usually has a *chavrusa*, but today his *chavrusa* will certainly forgive him if he cannot concentrate properly. After all, everyone knows that he sat and learned through the night. His afternoon *chavrusa* will have to forgive him if he goes to bed. It is no mean feat to sit and learn through the night. When he rises from his sweet sleep, he starts making calculations. The net result of his *hasmadah* has been the cancellation of two *chavrusos*. Woe to such calculations! You utter fool, you. The dog from the Roman marketplace only wants one fresh, appetizing roll! *You* don't appreciate the importance of a *chavrusa*, but the *yetzer hora* does.

What will be the final result? This is the *yetzer hora's* method. Today he says, "Cancel a *chavrusa* to learn through the night." Tomorrow, "Cancel a *chavrusa* to do a good deed." A day later he says, "Cancel a *chavrusa* for no reason at all." In the end, he says "Go and serve idols—close your Gemara altogether!"

Rav Chaim delivered a *shiur* in a certain yeshiva. After the *shiur*, one of the listeners asked a question. Rav Chaim thought for a moment and then answered, "A sluggard is not one who doesn't learn. A sluggard is one who doesn't think."

THREE

REBBE AND *TALMID*

THE DISTINCTION between the younger and older students in the Mir Yeshiva was pronounced. The younger students sat in the front rows of the *beis hamedrash*, and the older students, the elite of the yeshiva, sat in the back rows. Each row had its own status, and it wasn't easy to move from one row to another. Mir students would bitingly describe this arrangement with the words, "To move from one bench to another in the Mir Yeshiva was a mortal risk."

The status system was very carefully preserved. Not wishing to interfere with the accepted customs of the yeshiva, Rav Chaim adhered to it. Nevertheless, in the corner of the *mizrach* where Rav Chaim stood learning, there was always a mixed group of younger and older students who came to "talk in learning" with him or simply to gather inspiration from the energy of the combative talmudic discussion that always surrounded him.

He had a stormy temperament and phenomenal physical strength, which were apparent in both his appearance and movements. He could rarely sit in one place for any length of time, but would walk up and down between the rows, banging energetically on the *shtenders* and benches. Sometimes, during a passionate discussion, he would become so excited that he would jump over the benches. Such behavior was not an expression of absentminded passion, but a manifestation of the *ahavas haTorah* that burned within him. Rav Chaim studied Torah with his entire physical and spiritual being, as if he were constantly proclaiming "the word of *Hashem* is law."

Mir graduates remember a cold, stormy night when a high voice and strange knocking sound were heard from the street. Peeping out through cracks in the walls, the frightened *bochurim* tried to see what was happening. It was Rav Chaim walking up and down the dark streets of Mir repeating a gemara to himself in a loud voice. In his hands, he held a tree branch with which, in the tempest of his learning, he was whacking all the stones in his path. Like a whirlwind, he entered the *beis hamedrash* and sat down to learn, his fervor inspiring others to join him. He used to say, "One can learn better in a storm than in quiet, for when one learns in quiet, one sleeps." (*Az iss shturemt in lernen lernt zich az menn zitst shtil shlaft zich.*)

The status distinctions so pronounced inside the *beis hamedrash* were nonexistent outside. In his dormitory room, Rav Chaim learned with younger *bochurim*. There all distinctions and divisions fell away; there he learned with *chavrusos* from whom he could receive and to whom he could give maximum spiritual benefit. He once remarked to one of his friends, "I am involved in nothing but learning. What other act of kindness can I do for my fellow man than learn with him as a *chavrusa?*" Knowing that it would enhance their status in the Mir, he was particularly eager to learn with graduates of Grodno Yeshiva.

Rav Chaim did not learn exclusively with gifted students, although it was not easy for him to learn with the less gifted; he had to bridge the gap somehow and establish some compatibility between these *chavrusos* and his amazing knowledge. The vehicles he used to make this possible were his wonderful *middos* and exceptional powers of explanation and clarification. His modesty, humility, and extraordinary systematic approach to learning brought him close to these *chavrusos*, and enabled him to help them understand complicated subject matter.

He could take apart any subject, break it down to its root components, and then concentrate on its central theme. He could unravel a subject's complexities and find its key points. Once he had identified the key point of any *sugya*, all the other surrounding details became general principles applicable anywhere in *Shass*. His method of analysis of the discussions in the Gemara and its commentaries would transform logical arguments into these principles, which were independently valid and could be utilized in any *sugya*. He formulated thousands of such principles and constantly strived to correlate them with all the material he had mastered. His students would describe this process by saying that "Every one of Rav Chaim's questions is based on a 'principle,' every answer is either based on another 'principle' or creates a 'principle.'"

His understanding was not limited to questions, answers, explanations, logical assumptions, and conclusions. He assumed that every detail in the Gemara had to be understood and approached in its own special way. He argued that the Torah scholars in each generation had their unique approach to learning and that they imparted this approach to their students. Yeshiva students are aware of these different approaches and can identify *chiddushei Torah* of later generations, saying, "This is the style of Rav Chaim Brisker (*Rav*

Chaimdik)....This is the style of Rav Shimon Shkop (*Rav Shimondik*)." But who can identify the approaches of the Sages of the talmudic era? Who can say, "This is *Rabbi Akivadik*, this is *Rabbi Tarfondik*"?

The Rambam could identify the approaches of the Sages of the Talmud. He knew what was *Rabbi Akivadik* and what was *Rabbi Tarfondik*. On the mishnah in *Pirkei Avos* [3:19], "Everything is foreseen, yet freedom of choice is given," the Rambam comments, "It was fitting for Rabbi Akiva to make a statement like this."

The Gemara [*Sukkah* 28a] says, "Rabbi Eliezer the Great never said anything he had not heard from his teacher." But in *Avos DeRabbi Noson* [6:3], is it not explicitly stated that when Rabbi Eliezer the Great was appointed *rosh yeshiva*, he uttered wonderful ideas that no one had ever heard before? If the Mishnah says he uttered "ideas that no one had ever heard," it must mean that Rabbi Eliezer the Great had also never heard them. The question is twofold. First, it says he never said anything he had not heard from his teacher. Second, everybody knows that one who learns always creates *chiddushim*. Is it possible that Rav Eliezer the Great did not say anything new, or even refrained from saying *chiddushim* because he had not heard them from his teacher?

The answer is obvious. Every child knows that Rabbi Eliezer the Great must have created *chiddushim* that had not been said by his teacher. If so, what does the Mishnah mean by "[He] never said anything he had not heard from his teacher"? It means he never said anything his teacher would not have said. The definition of a *talmid* is a student who knows what his rebbe would have said in any given situation.

It is frightening! Because every rebbe has a unique approach, every *talmid* must ask himself, "What would my rebbe have said about this?" If the student grasps this approach, he deserves to be called a *talmid*; if not, he does not deserve to be called a *talmid*. One who cannot say what his rebbe would have said, but only what his rebbe actually said, is not a *talmid*. He is a tape recorder!

Now you can understand how a person can say things no one has ever heard, yet only say what he heard from his rebbe. In every line of Gemara that Rav Eliezer the Great learned he heard the voice of his rebbe.

Rav Chaim extended this even further, maintaining that every *seder* of *Shass* had its own unique approach, which distinguishes it from other *sedarim*. The Gemara (*Bava Metzia* 109b) relates that a student once asked Rav Ashi a question, and Rav Ashi answered, "Ask me this question when we learn *Kodashim*." Rav Chaim found an explanation for Rav Ashi's answer in the *Shittah Mekubetzes*. Rav Ashi's answer— the approach to learning which would furnish an answer to this question—is not the approach of *Nezikin*. This student's question should only be asked when learning *Kodashim*. Rav Chaim added, "There are many good questions to which the answer is found in *Nega'im* and *Oholos*. Here is not the place for such a question."

This same concept was a firm guideline for discussing the study of *mussar*. He was strongly opposed to a strictly halachic approach to analyzing *maamorei Chazal*. He believed that the *mussar* sayings of *Chazal* needed a different approach, and in one of his *shmuessen*, he summed this up referring to the *Shittah Mekubetzes*: "This is my answer to those who have certain questions on my *mussar shmuessen*."

One can assume that at the spiritual height at which Rav Chaim lived, there must have been elevated moments that filled him with joy. Nevertheless, Rav Chaim talked about only two such moments. About one he said, "It was the happiest night of my life," and about the other, "It was the happiest day of my life."

One occurred during a journey in Poland. He arrived in a certain town late at night and slept in the house of a Mir graduate. As was his custom, Rav Chaim discussed Torah with his host and presented a particular *mussar* idea. His host sat listening to him with his eyes closed. Rav Chaim said, "If you are tired and want to sleep, I won't bore you with my talking." His host answered, "No, please continue," then closed his eyes again. Rav Chaim continued to develop his idea, still suspecting that his host didn't really want to listen to him. "Don't disturb yourself," said Rav Chaim. "If you want to sleep, go to bed." His host opened his eyes and, with a look of joy, answered him, "No, I'm not tired. It's just that when I close my eyes, I hear our rebbe, Rav Yeruchem, talking."

"That was the happiest night of my life," Rav Chaim told his students.

The other concerned a *talmid* who told Rav Chaim a *chiddush* that was in fact was one of Rav Chaim's:

Do you really think he had the nerve to be telling me that my *shiur* was his *chiddush?* Of course not. He must have heard the *shiur*, forgotten it, and learned the subject matter again, exactly as I learned it....

I had a *talmid*! It was the happiest day of my life.

*   *   *

Rav Chaim's concept of "order" in learning was far-reaching, and its source was firmly rooted in his own personality, for order reigned supreme in all his acts and deeds. His dress was tidy, his handwriting neat, his daily schedule was extremely well organized. Even the smallest, most mundane detail of his daily life was carefully arranged. Students even expressed admiration at how neatly Rav Chaim wrote a postcard. He was especially fastidious about the order of the books in his bookcase, which he himself would arrange.

He wrote out the *shiurim* he gave at the Mir Yeshiva in thick, wide exercise books. They were written out without any preliminary drafts in a very clear hand. Not one word was crossed out. If he made a mistake, which rarely happened because of his self-discipline, he did not cross it out, but put an asterisk next to it and wrote in the margin, "Should read..."

In *mussar shmuessen* which he gave in later years, Rav Chaim taught that organization and orderliness have to be internalized until they become basic character traits, a second nature. At the beginning of a *zman*, he once spoke on the significance of *sedarim* in a yeshiva. In the same *shmuess*, he elaborated on the concepts of the organization of creation and the exact placement of every minute detail in it.

The time of *seder* has arrived. *Sedarim* determine how, when, and where things should be done. *Seder* has started, and at a time when he shouldn't be there, a *bochur* is still in his room. The room is topsy-turvy—*something* is not in the right place at the right time. The order of the room has been disturbed.

*   *   *

Sometimes there would be two distinct and even opposing opinions which explained a *sugya*. Rav Chaim would bring many proofs for one opinion, proofs so solid that his *chavrusa* would be absolutely convinced that this was the only way to understand the *sugya*. Then he would produce an equally long list of proofs for the second opinion. His confused *chavrusa* would believe that both opinions were equally valid; he could not see any way to choose between them. At this point, Rav Chaim would use his own unique method of determining which opinion was correct. He would, as it were, place them on the scales of his total Torah knowledge and determine that, in *his* opinion, one option was more acceptable than the other.

Sometimes he would advance a *chiddush* and strengthen it with numerous proofs that seemed to indicate it must be true, only to shake his head and say, "It appears to me that this *chiddush* is not true...." On many occasions, his *chiddush* contradicted practical, accepted halachic rulings. He would then search for a way to disprove his proofs, sometimes without success. Rav Chaim tried very hard not to arrive at any practical halachic conclusions. When it came to *halacha lemaaseh*, he would say, "This should be referred to a Rav. I don't know if he knows, but it's his expertise."

His genius allowed him to survey a single subject at one time from many different and even contradictory perspectives. It was difficult to find absolute conclusions in his approach. He maintained that when it comes to the study of Torah, one has to prove the truth of many approaches because all of them may indeed be true. The method of *chakiros* was not accepted by him. He did not always see the necessity of selecting one option at the expense of another. "Why one or the other? What's wrong with both?" he would often ask. He could devote an entire *shiur* to proving that one could just as easily choose the other option. A student once asked about a particular subject, "Is it this or is it that?" Amused, Rav Chaim answered, "Choose whichever is more convenient for you!" *(Kleibzich vos iz dir bakvemer!)*

Rav Chaim made every effort to ensure that his *chavrusos* should not be "passive partners." He would encourage them in every possible way, building their confidence in their ability to achieve. He often "fooled" them into thinking that they were actually arriving at the *chiddushim* themselves. He had a knack of presenting a subject in its entirety up to the final point, then letting them resolve it, which gave them the sweet taste of saying *chiddushim.*

One cannot measure the benefit his *chavrusos* derived from learning with him. In clever ways, he fashioned their talents, developed their understanding, and broadened their knowledge. In his company, they learned about living Torah, not just knowledge of Torah. They learned the way of Torah and how to acquire it. They saw his tremendous efforts in Torah learning, his endless patience, and his humility. In his company, it was not possible to consider lessening one's concentration for even a second. His life may be epitomized by a comment he once made to his *chavrusa* when someone knocked on the door of his room: "If he is coming to do me a favor, the biggest favor he can do is to allow me to learn undisturbed."

His whole essence was *zrizus*, something which was most obvious when he learned. Time and time again, with tireless patience, he would review unclear points that he had come across until they became clear. In his room in the Mir, there was a sofa on which he would half sit and half recline as he immersed himself in concentrated thought. His face would burn with the effort, and he would perspire heavily. The veins in his forehead would look as if they were about to burst. His *ahavas haTorah* was contagious, and those in his company became accustomed to continuous exertion in Torah study.

One freezing winter day, he came to learn wrapped in a fur coat. The building was unheated, but the excitement of his learning and the labor of his concentration warmed him so that his whole body began to perspire. First, he removed his coat, then his jacket, then as he became more involved in the heat of learning, he removed his sweater, continuing to learn in a thin shirt.

On another occasion, Rav Chaim was learning *Yerushalmi* with a *chavrusa* until late at night, and they worked out seven or eight ways of understanding the *sugya*. The following day, in his usual manner, he summed up the previous day's learning precisely, repeating all the different approaches they had discussed. His *chavrusa*, who himself was one of the most learned students in the Mir, was disturbed. "How can you remember everything so well?" he asked, "I don't remember anything." Rav Chaim answered, "What did you do last night after we finished learning?" The *chavrusa* answered, "I went to bed." "And I," said Rav Chaim, "got into bed, with my head face downward under my pillow so as not to wake up my roommate, and shouted over and over for a few hours all the different approaches to the *sugya* in order to knock them into my head. It's no wonder that I remember."

Once he mentioned that he had fourteen questions on the subject at hand, and, in his usual manner, started listing them. When he could not remember one of the questions, his *chavrusa* was satisfied with thirteen, but Rav Chaim would not compromise. He reviewed his summation again and again until he fished the fourteenth question out of his memory.

Such stories demonstrated to his *chavrusos-talmidim* the important combination of learning, revision, patience, and willpower. The methodology of dividing subjects into questions, principles, answers, and summations taught an important lesson in how to create internal organization in one's learning. Only after completing interim summations down to the smallest details would he continue learning.

Perhaps Rav Chaim's *simchah*, more than anything else, infected everyone around him with *ahavas haTorah*.

The days of Purim are established as days of feasting and rejoicing. This is difficult—these are days of *kabolas haTorah*, and, therefore, they should have been established as days of meditation and seriousness. The explanation is that *simchah* is such that it draws people near to one another. The condition for receiving the Torah is " 'They encamped'—as one man with one heart," which can only be achieved through *simchah*.

When he was learning, Rav Chaim would seemingly melt with *simchah*. A smile always hovered at the corners of his lips. Notwithstanding his seriousness and tremendous concentration, he abounded with tireless excitement and energy. He used many different expressions of *simchah* in the course of learning, some of which can only be appreciated in their original Yiddish. These expressions—witty and sharp plays on words—were infectious and created a happy, alert atmosphere. Many comments about *sevaros* were full of incisive and lively humor. Concerning an acceptable *sevora*, he would eloquently proclaim, "It is 'sweeter than tar'. " Concerning a point that had been clarified he would say, "It is *sossondik* [or *simchadik*]."

A *chavrusa* relates his experience learning *Taharos* with Rav Chaim in the women's gallery of the Kaidan Yeshiva. Rav Chaim found a link between what they were learning and a certain topic in *Bava Kama*. In his enthusiasm, he stood up on the bench. Then, when he had arranged his thoughts and was absolutely certain they were correct, he stood up on the table, and his feet started to dance, as if of their own accord, as he repeated, over and over, the *chiddush* he had discovered.

Entire worlds of careful attention, self-control, and developed *middos* were revealed in him when he learned. With his special regard for his *chavrusos*, his behavior towards them contained not a grain of pride or arrogance. He was known to be tough and quick when he had to rebuke someone, but it was always with a gentle aside, or in a roundabout, hinting manner, so the person would not be offended. Even after he became the *rosh yeshiva* in Yerushalayim, Rav Chaim still would decide what to learn with his *chavrusos* only after "seeking advice" from them. When a young *bochur* wanted to join a *chavrusa* with him, Rav Chaim answered that he had to get permission from the other *chavrusa*, who was also a young *bochur*.

He would refer to a *chavrusa* with the fond nickname *bruderke*, brother (the suffix denotes fondness). It might have been thought that this was simply an acquired style of speaking, but one impression is consistent in all the reminiscences of Mir Yeshiva graduates, and it inspires a smile of yearning in the sea of pain that these memories arouse: Rav Chaim was a good brother. (*Rav Chaim iz givveyn a gutter bruder.*)

Rav Yehudah said, The only reason I am sharper than my colleagues is that I saw the back of Rav Meir.

(Eruvin 13b)

During the course of the year I maintain (let it not be said about you) that I am a simple person. But today, the *yahrzeit* of my rebbe, Rav Yeruchem, I must not say this. Today, I must say the only reason I am sharper than my colleagues is that I saw the back of Rav Yeruchem.

(Rav Chaim Shmulevitz)

FOUR

THE *MAGGID SHIUR*

R AV YERUCHEM, *mashgiach* of the Mir Yeshiva in those years, discovered in Rav Chaim an unusual personality of limitless spiritual potential. He was deeply fond of him, and his relationship with Rav Chaim was different from his relationships with the other *talmidim* in the yeshiva. Rav Yeruchem's close friendship with Rav Alter, Rav Chaim's late father, also played a role in this special affinity.

Rav Yeruchem was constantly surrounded by groups of *talmidim* to whom he would impart his teachings. On rare occasions, when there were personal issues to be discussed, he would talk with an individual privately. He treated Rav Chaim differently. Rav Chaim would spend every Shabbos in Rav Yeruchem's home, and every *motzo'ei* Shabbos, a few hours after he had delivered his *shmuess*, he would closet himself in his room with Rav Chaim and ask him to review everything he had learned that week. They would then continue, discussing *mussar* and *machshavah* topics. Rav Chaim received many personal guidelines and directives from Rav Yeruchem.

It was Rav Yeruchem who said about him, "Rav Chaim 'Stutchiner' does not need *mussar*; he can achieve the same results with his Torah study."

Rav Chaim was well aware of his unusual capabilities and the enormous potential that lay within his wealth of knowledge. He had dreamt in his youth of "revolutionizing the world" by constructing entirely novel approaches to Torah study. This self-awareness notwithstanding, Rav Chaim often proclaimed that if he was unique in any way, it was only the result of the education he had received from his teachers. We have no way of knowing how Rav Chaim perceived the spiritual factors that had molded him, but one thing is clear, he was well aware of these factors and was proficient enough at self-analysis to determine the causes of his progress and achievements. Despite the fact Rav Chaim had been in a class by himself in Stutchin and Grodno, he still felt he had gained a special dimension from his relationship with Rav Yeruchem. Whenever he remembered Rav Yeruchem, he did not hesitate to reveal his deep feelings: "I am sharper than my colleagues, because I saw the back of Rav Yeruchem."

The Gaon Rav Eliezer Yehudah Finkel, the *rosh yeshiva* of the Mir throughout its glorious years in Poland, spared no effort to foster a very special atmosphere in the yeshiva, one which generated a burning ambition for spiritual growth. Drawing from his own brilliance in Torah and *mussar*, and his spiritual greatness, he originated many and varied techniques to encourage and inspire scholastic rivalry. He carefully cultivated a setting in which the yardstick of achievement was *Shass*—to have hundreds of pages of Gemara, *Rashi,* and *Tosafos* committed to memory—and a desire to grow and be innovative in Torah. His close personal contact with his students did not allow any of them to hide in a corner—all were involved in the challenge. Rav Eliezer Yehudah regularly provoked them to be innovative and progressive. During his tenure as *rosh yeshiva*, the Mir gained fame and renown; it drew the most outstanding Torah scholars of the Jewish world, for many years molding an entire generation of outstanding *talmidim*. But despite the eminence of the Mir student body, Rav Chaim's position remained unique.

The life of Rav Eliezer Yehudah Finkel was involved with Rav Chaim's for many years. He was not only his rebbe and mentor, and a *godol beYisroel*, but he also became his father-in-law. Rav Chaim saw in Rav "Laizer Yudel" a giant from a previous generation, and he revered him deeply. To Rav Chaim, Rav Laizer Yudel's personality and Torah knowledge represented ultimate greatness. When Rav Laizer Yudel passed away in 1965, Rav Chaim's *hesped,* punctuated with heart-rending cries and fiery speech, shook all present. He summed up the depth of his esteem for his father-in-law in one short sentence: "I cannot comprehend the greatness of the *rishonim*. My comprehension stops at the *rosh yeshiva*."

It was Rav Yeruchem who suggested that Rav Chaim marry Rav Laizer Yudel's only daughter. She had absorbed her father's great love of Torah, and in addition to her common sense and intelligence, she was famous for a distinguished and noble character. In 1930, Rav Chaim married the *rosh yeshiva's* daughter, who was to be his faithful companion, constantly at his side. In times of trouble, distress, illness, and hardship, recognizing his greatness, she sacrificed herself completely for his study of Torah. In the bitter days of the Shanghai *golus*, when he was drowning in dangers and troubles, Rav Chaim once groaned to her, "All this will result in my becoming an *am haaretz*." "You will have to toil many, many years to become an *am haaretz*," she comforted him.

When the *shidduch* was suggested, the five years that Rav Laizer Yudel had already known him and the closeness of their relationship did not help in the slightest. For six weeks, everyday Rav Chaim went to Rav Laizer Yudel to tell him his *chiddushim*. Each day he would present his future father-in-law with twelve or more varied comments on different *sugyos* in *Shass*. This "test" convinced the *rosh yeshiva* that the *illuy* from Stutchin was indeed suitable for his daughter.

At the end of his life, Rav Laizer Yudel departed from his customary behavior and praised his son-in-law. He pointed out, with obvious admiration, how impressed he had been during those six weeks with the fact that Rav Chaim was able to keep separate in his mind the twelve different topics they discussed each day, and how amazed he was with the orderliness of Rav Chaim's thought and his familiarity with each and every *sugya*.

Some insight into the deep esteem in which he held his son-in-law can be gleaned from the following story. The *Vaad Hayeshivos* met to eulogize one of the *gedolei Yisroel*. Rav Chaim, who was among the *maspidim*, mentioned Avrohom's *hesped* on Sarah.

If the Torah writes, "Avrohom came to eulogize Sarah and to weep for her," the *posuk* must contain some indication of the content of the *hesped*. The previous *posuk* states, "The life of Sarah was one hundred years and twenty years and seven years, these were the years of Sarah's life." Rashi comments, "All the years were alike in goodness." Sarah's spiritual progress was uninterrupted. Avrohom's perception was not as great as Sarah's, for he was second to her in prophecy. Nonetheless, his *hesped* was the epitome of perception, for it contained the concept of continuity— a life that is one spiritual progression. How does one make one's life an unbroken continuity of spiritual development?

It takes fifteen minutes to boil a kettle of water. If we heat the kettle a hundred times, for only fourteen minutes each time, the water remains unboiled, yet with one fifteen-minute boiling the water becomes a new reality—boiled water. Until a person reaches his spiritual boiling point, his progress is fragmented, alternately hot and cold, so his essence remains unchanged. When, however, through effort and exertion, he reaches a boiling point in *avodas Hashem*, he will remain there infinitely, for he has become a new reality.

As Rav Chaim continued with words of praise about the deceased, whose entire life had been one of unbroken spiritual progress, Rav Laizer Yudel whispered to his neighbor, "Rav Chaim is talking about himself."

*   *   *

One of the great roshei yeshiva *used to say, "I will be released from punishment after death for I have received my punishment in this world watching* talmidim *run away when I come to say a* shiur." *I would not go so far, but seeing* talmidim *run away from a* shiur *is not easy. How can one come to terms with this?*
(Rav Chaim Shmulevitz)

For the first six years of his marriage, Rav Chaim continued on his path with great momentum. There was no difference between the intensity of his learning when he was a bachelor and the intensity of his learning after he was married and took on family commitments. He continued his daily schedule of uninterrupted *chavrusos* and was financially supported by his father-in-law.

In 1936, he began to say *shiurim* in the Mir. Contrary to custom, the entire student body of the yeshiva, young *bochurim* and old, came to hear his first *shiur*, an obvious expression of the esteem in which he was held. Although their expectations had been high before the *shiur*, the listeners reacted to it with even greater excitement. The *shiur's* unique structure and scope, the concise and clear division of ideas, and the eloquence with which it was delivered all combined to leave an indelible impression on the audience. The subject was the *Tosafos* at the beginning of *Bava Basra*. Rav Chaim commenced with four seemingly unrelated questions. He then brought to light a number of fundamental principles. The clarification and structuring of these principles was clearly in the style of his rebbe, Rav Shimon Shkop. With the flashes of genius so typical of his style, Rav Chaim connected the four questions using these principles and answered them with one answer. He did not leave it at that, but proved these principles with a wealth of sources. After the *shiur*, everyone agreed that, although it had not taken longer than the customary hour, its content could have sufficed for five or more *shiurim*. The *shiur* was crammed with valuable information, yet its order and the numerous summations made it easily understandable and retainable down to the smallest detail. This first *shiur* was the prototype of the thousands of *shiurim* Rav Chaim was to give for nearly fifty years.

The content and presentation of his *shiurim* were very different from his style and method of learning. The *chiddushim* he created while learning with a *chavrusa* were the products of intense concentration, exertion, and methodical repetition of each word and group of words, yet they almost seemed to be by-products of his physical and spiritual hard labor. With a *chavrusa*, Rav Chaim would explain every concept in a number of ways, each one based on proofs so solid that it appeared this was the *only* way the concept could be understood. Because *truth* was the cornerstone of his approach to learning, he had to prove that each and every way he explained a concept was the only way to shed light on the *sugya*. His *chiddushim* were expounded in a decisive manner— *the truth.*

Rav Chaim's *shiurim* were much different. He never approached a *sugya* from a firm or fixed viewpoint, but appeared to create his own viewpoint during the course of the *shiur*. No single *chiddush* was presented as the only way to understand the *sugya*. Rather, flashes of genius and original creativity accompanied an obvious desire to arouse the listeners' interest. One of his *talmidim* described his *shiurim* by saying, "The *shiurim* were in the main *charifus* and *pilpul*. They did not concentrate on 'what has to be said here' but rather on 'how to arrive at what has to be said.'" Those familiar with his *derech halimud* were amazed at the flexibility of his mind, how he could change his style so completely from *chavrusa* to *shiur*. To show "how to arrive at what has to be said" demanded that the *shiur* teach a *derech halimud* which gave the student the means to distinguish between seemingly similar points. The presentation of facts had to follow a very specific sequence, one in which even the smallest detail was positioned for maximum clarity. Rav Chaim succeeded in achieving all of this, and the sequencing of questions, proofs, and principles transformed the *shiur* into a wellspring of creative thinking.

Rav Chaim found presenting a *shiur* most difficult. By nature he was very shy, and although he did not suffer from stage fright, he lacked a spontaneous rapport with his audience. In his early years, this problem was manifested in the difficulty he had lecturing on aggada. In Grodno, he felt jealous of those who could easily speak at *simchos* and festive occasions. It was not that he lacked material, for by that time he already had a remarkable storehouse of aggadic insights. Rather, he felt that his personality and nature were not suited

to draw the hearts of his listeners close to him. In the course
of his teaching in the Grodno Yeshiva, he concluded that even
when the audience suited his temperament and was thirsty for
knowledge, the material had to be presented in a manner
particularly suited to that audience. Therefore, although he did
not naturally possess any of the techniques needed to deliver
a *shiur* in a way that would ensure his audience's understanding, he concentrated on developing them. Despite all
these efforts, he never overcame his natural shyness and
always said a *shiur* with his eyes closed. The first *shiur* of a
new *zman* always made him nervous.

Over the years, he found many sources in *Chazal, rishonim,*
and *acharonim* emphasizing the importance of pedagogical
techniques. We are taught (*Chullin* 63b) that one should always
teach *talmidim* in a concise way. In later years, Rav Chaim
gave a detailed presentation expounding the Rambam's understanding of this principle. He found numerous sayings of
Chazal and halachic rulings from the *Rambam* and *Shulchan
Aruch* that were based on the principle that a *talmid* has the
right to understand and a teacher the *obligation* to explain and
clarify. He once discovered a remarkable *chiddush* in halacha:
it is permissible to present totally hypothetical situations and
pose hypothetical questions simply to sharpen the minds of
talmidim. He then showed that the halacha clearly defines how
this may be done and to what extent. Rav Chaim also found
halachic rulings that gave detailed advice on how to explain
material to *talmidim,* and to what extent a teacher is obligated
to clarify material and to provoke the *talmidim* so they
themselves arrive at a correct understanding without it being
handed to them on a plate. In effect, he had discovered the
equivalent of a detailed *Shulchan Aruch* on a teacher's obligations; it had reference to the teacher's spiritual level and also
presented detailed techniques of teaching used by Torah
scholars throughout the ages.

He prepared his *shiurim* with a *chavrusa* and would often exclaim, "How does one fulfill one's obligation?" (*Gevald vi iz men yoitze?*) He offered many proofs, however—without a proof a theory is worthless—to support the theory that a *talmid*'s understanding of a *shiur* is not always dependent on the teacher's presentation. The *talmid* first has to be fashioned into a "utensil." One of these proofs was the story told in *Bava Kama* (20b) about Rami Bar Chanina who asked a friend to render a service in order to strengthen the friend's attitude of *bittul* toward him as rebbe. He did this only to help the friend understand the material Rami Bar Chanina was about to teach him!

When learning with a *chavrusa*, Rav Chaim was able to discern the *chavrusa's* individual abilities and disposition and respond accordingly. The presentation of a public *shiur*, however, presented great difficulty because of the varying capabilities of the audience. A *sevara* that only part of the audience could understand could not be used; he did not feel he had fulfilled his obligation if only some of the audience understood him. When preparing a *shiur* together with his *chavrusa*, he sometimes found that he could not produce a construction that was clear, convincing, and interesting. At such times, he would turn to his *chavrusa* and say in a pleading tone, "Here is the entire subject laid out in front of you. Use your talents and turn it into something I can say in the *shiur*."

He felt no qualms at saying two *shiurim* that seemed contradictory, maintaining that this served to sharpen the minds of the *talmidim*. Once, when someone pointed out to him that the *shiur* he had just said was moving in a direction totally contradictory to the previous *shiur*, he retorted, "What do you care?"

He was sensitive to anything that would diminish the concentration of his audience or their patience. He never went beyond the time allotted for a *shiur* because he was well aware that the eyes of the audience would begin to wander to the clock once the time limit had been reached. He never realized how upset everyone was when the clock showed that a *shiur* would have to end. Once, when a newly appointed *rosh yeshiva* finished saying his first public *shiur*, the *talmidim* gathered around him to ask questions. Rav Chaim also went over to comment, "You overran the time allotted to you!" He believed that the listener had to know in advance how long a *shiur* would last in order to be able to organize his schedule, for he did not understand how one could go through the day without having a fixed schedule. He once commented to a *rosh yeshiva* who had a daily *chavrusa* for an indeterminate amount of time, "A *chavrusa* without a fixed time frame is *avodas perech* (hard labor)."

Rav Chaim would prepare a *shiur* by saying it out loud to himself exactly as he planned to deliver it in public. If he was not satisfied with the way it sounded, he would not hesitate to change the presentation radically. He even planned in advance when he would raise or lower his voice, when he would stand still or move around, and at what point he would bang on the *shtender* for emphasis. He also knew when he would pause to allow the audience time to digest what he had said and heighten the tension. He made great use of physical gestures to emphasize his points.

*　　　*　　　*

The chachomim *commanded us, saying, "Anyone who talks too much brings sin." It is also said, "I have found nothing better for myself than silence." So also in Torah and* divrei chochmah *we find that a person's words should be few but their content great. This is what the* chachomim *commanded us, saying that a person should always teach his* talmidim *in a concise manner. But if one's words are many and their content little, this is foolishness.*

(Rambam, Hilchos De'os 2:4)

Nu, *who wants to be a fool?*

(Rav Chaim Shmulevitz)

In general, Rav Chaim began a *shiur* with four questions in ascending order of difficulty. He would proceed to establish fundamental principles, usually four, and then explain the flow of the *sugya*. After suggesting a single answer that synthesized all the principles he had mentioned, he would then use it to deal with all the questions.

He would conclude each section of a *shiur* with a phrase such as "Up to this point the questions..." "Until here the principles..." "*Nu*, what do we have so far?" or "This was an introduction." After every such statement, he would briefly summarize what he had already said and then move on to the next section, continuing to comment along the way, "Up to here is the first third [quarter, half] of the *shiur*." After each such comment, he would again summarize. In this way, he would summarize a *shiur* many times, expressing himself in a different manner each time so as not to bore the audience. This not only helped the listeners remember the *shiur*, but also educated them in the importance of repetition and review.

Despite the seriousness with which he approached a *shiur*, he was not loathe to present a *sevara* with irony or make a humorous comment which he felt would awaken his listeners. If Rav Chaim thought that the subject matter could be explained more clearly by altering the normal structure of his presentation, he would not hesitate to do so. There were occasions when he changed the structure simply to surprise the audience and arouse their attention and interest.

He was constantly guided by the words of the Vilna Gaon: "Shlomo HaMelech said, 'In all labor there is profit, but the talk of the lips leads only to loss' [Mishlei 14:23]. Shlomo HaMelech taught us a general rule—too much talk can only result in a loss. Even when explaining to others, the speaker should minimize his speech so the listener can analyze his words and add his own conception to them. This is what the verse means. 'In all labor there is profit...'—if you minimize your words, the listener profits by laboring to establish what you mean. 'But the talk of the lips...'—if you amplify your words, you deter the listener from laboring to understand them and cause him to concentrate on trying to contradict you" (Vilna Gaon, in his commentary on the Siddur).

Rav Chaim excelled in the use of brief sentences. He would occasionally break off in the middle of a sentence, leaving the audience to complete it in their minds. He would present an entire shiur, leaving the final connections and conclusions to the imagination of the audience. One of his favorite expressions was "I have to make the other person a partner in what I'm saying." In this way, he encouraged his talmidim to believe they had the ability to understand and even add to what their rebbe had said.

He considered adding to one's knowledge to be one of the forty-eight ways of acquiring Torah listed in Pirkei Avos (6:6)—"listening and adding." The shiur was a cornerstone of the learning process, and, therefore, the ability to "listen and add" had to be inculcated in the talmidim through the shiur.

His shiurim were superbly well ordered and easily understood; but, when others, even scholars, would try to repeat one, they would find it necessary to make lengthy introductions just to bring the listeners to Rav Chaim's starting point.

His *shiurim* never included any superfluous information. And although the content of a single one could have sufficed for five, he succeeded in summarizing each *shiur* in the last five minutes. In these brief summaries, he never missed an essential detail.

Rav Chaim never articulated the educational theories that gave rise to the structure of his *shiurim*, but his spontaneous comments often revealed them. A certain *maggid shiur*, who was a respected *talmid chochom*, was not successful in delivering *shiurim*. His inherent honesty did not allow him to make a great fuss about any question to which he thought he had an answer. This lack of dramatic emphasis often resulted in his questions and answers being lost in his explanation of the *sugya*. His *shiurim* gave an overall impression of lack of order and clarity. Rav Chaim advised the *maggid shiur*, "When you ask a question, say it with such conviction that at that moment you yourself truly believe that it has no answer."

Those who did not know him well may have assumed that his *shiurim* were the ultimate expression of his greatness in Torah. But those who were close to him and aware of the sharp difference between his approach to saying a *shiur* and learning with a *chavrusa* knew better. The *shiurim* themselves did not demonstrate his Torah greatness; they did serve, however, to demonstrate the greatness of his *middos* and his constant effort to excel spiritually in areas totally ignored by others. Once he let slip a "hidden" dimension of his understanding of how to give *shiurim* when he told a *rosh yeshiva*, a former *chavrusa* of his, "One who truly understands the whole idea of giving a *shiur* understands that it involves a great deal of *bein odom l'chavero.*"

From Rav Yeruchem, Rav Chaim inherited the tradition of preparing a new *shiur* every week. His preparation for a single *shiur* could have sufficed for many weeks, but, faithful to the *mashgiach's* instructions, he always prepared a new one, even if he still had something to say from the previous week.

Every *chiddush* that occurred to him while he was learning with his *chavrusos* he wrote down. He had a fixed time for writing and tried very hard never to delay it. Once, when he was found writing at an unusual time, he explained, "I owe myself writing time." He wrote his *chiddushim* on pieces of paper which he would fold and cut to make his own notebook. Later, when preparing the *shiur* with his *chavrusa*, he would review his notes and decide which were suitable.

He firmly believed that the extent of his *talmidim*'s efforts to understand his *shiurim* depended on their awareness of how much effort he had expended in preparation. He was well aware of the esteem in which he was held and feared that the *talmidim* might think that he did not need to prepare his *shiurim* because of his knowledge and genius. He feared they might think that the ideas in the *shiurim* came up, as it were, by the way, while he was learning, or that he was repeating old *shiurim*. Therefore, when the *bochurim* in the Mir started to say *chaburos*, Rav Chaim was thrilled: "Only one who has once said, 'I made, I expended effort, I toiled,' can begin to appreciate how difficult it is to prepare a *dvar Torah* to say in public."

Although each *shiur's* content and structure were the result of extreme physical and spiritual effort, he never complimented himself, but always maintained that the secret of his successful *shiurim* was his *chavrusos*. When one of his *chavrusos* died, Rav Chaim eulogized him, saying, "My *shiurim* are in fact his."

Rav Chaim taught Torah in the Mir in Poland for four years, after many years of continuous learning of varied subjects with many different *bochurim*. Indeed, it sometimes appeared as if Rav Chaim had his own little yeshiva amidst the greater Mir and that his four years of giving *shiurim* were just another aspect of his activities in spreading Torah. During these years, he managed to give *shiurim* on complete cycles of *masechtos* and establish thousands of talmudic principles. Those who listened to him faithfully not only received a wealth of knowledge but also a fundamental, in-depth understanding of key *sugyos* in *Shass*. Even those who were not close to him and did not regularly attend all his *shiurim* admit to receiving a basic education from Rav Chaim in the methodology of the study of Gemara.

Graduates from those years emphatically insist that anyone who came in contact with Rav Chaim advanced in his learning and *hasmadah* and that those who were really close to him, even if they were not particularly studious, became serious scholars in a short time.

One graduate, a respected *bochur* in the Mir, who later published a *sefer* of *chiddushei Torah*, writes in his introduction: "...and also my Teacher and Rebbe, our Master, the *Rosh Yeshiva*, his Honor, the renowned Gaon and Torah Prince, the Gaon Rav Chaim Shmulevitz. Whoever merited to absorb from the breadth of his Torah can never again experience any limitations in Torah study or small mindedness...."

"Grace is deceitful" refers to the generation of Moshe and Yehoshua; "and beauty is vain" refers to the generation of Chizkiya; "while she that fears the Lord shall be praised" refers to the generation of Rav Yehudah, the son of Rav Illai, of whose time it was said, "The poverty was so great that six of his disciples had to cover themselves with one garment between them, yet they studied the Torah."

(*Sanhedrin* 20a)

It is advantageous to study Torah in times of stress not just because of the spiritual reward, but because the Torah studied at such times is superior. The facts support this and prove it. The *chiddushim* the Shaagas Aryeh wrote during his wanderings are far superior to those he wrote in times of calmness.

(Rav Chaim Shmulevitz)

FIVE

GOLUS

THE SECOND WORLD WAR erupted in late 1939. In a secret agreement signed between Germany and Russia, Poland was divided between them. After the German army occupied half of Poland, the Red Army crossed the eastern border, and within a few days—the day after Rosh Hashanah 5700—the town of Mir came under Communist control. The Soviets, who wanted to exile the yeshiva en masse to Siberia, "advised" its administration not to disperse the *bochurim*. There seemed to be no way out. The Communists viewed the teachers and students of the yeshiva as counter-revolutionaries, and for this the sentence was either exile to Siberia or "the wall." There was seemingly no hope of the yeshiva escaping to the area outside of Russian control.

The Russian-German agreement contained a strange clause. Vilna, the capital of Lithuania, had been invaded by Poland in 1920 and incorporated into the Republic of Poland in 1923. The agreement which divided Poland granted Lithuania the right to her capital Vilna. Thus, Russian-occupied Vilna would be returned to Lithuania.

This clause was to provide an amazing escape route. Travel from Mir to Vilna was relatively trouble free at the time, since they were both Russian-occupied, and from Vilna one could enter the part of Lithuania which had not been invaded yet. With heavy hearts, half expecting a Russian trap, the yeshiva took up its wandering staff. In the middle of the night, after secret, hasty arrangements had been made, it set off on its first voyage on the sea of suffering that was to be its milieu for years to come. The yeshiva administration remained temporarily in Mir and only joined the hundreds of exiled *talmidim* a few days later.

The circumstances surrounding the organization of the departure from Mir contained a lesson that Rav Chaim would talk about in later years:

> It was necessary to leave...but all were troubled by the question, how does one leave home? While everything still stood in its proper place, no one dared to make the first move....I grabbed a table and moved it to the far end of the room....Then they started to move....

They entered Vilna without problems. Those who tarried in Mir later had to smuggle themselves across a new Lithuanian-Russian border.

When the Polish army collapsed, those yeshiva *bochurim* who had been drafted found themselves wandering aimlessly across occupied Poland. They removed their uniforms and, at great risk, made every possible effort to join the yeshiva in Vilna. One of these *bochurim*, who had learned *chavrusa* with Rav Chaim, was wandering through the streets of Vilna trying to find where the yeshiva had settled. He was dressed strangely in a variety of discarded garments picked up in different shuls. Finally he chanced on Rav Chaim. The *bochur*, today a *mashgiach* in a yeshiva, pointed out that, despite his very strange appearance, Rav Chaim immediately recognized him and fell on him with great excitement, as if he had found a long-lost brother.

The first stop that the yeshiva made in Vilna was the Ramailles Yeshiva building, but it was too small to house three hundred and fifty Mir students. Later, when Vilna was taken over by the Lithuanians, the yeshiva moved to the larger Novgorod Synagogue, named after the Vilna suburb in which it was situated.

Two weeks after the yeshiva arrived in Vilna, the Russians left, returning the city to the Lithuanians. The two-week delay in the arrival of the Lithuanian army in Vilna allowed free entry into the city for thousands of additional refugees. These thousands of displaced persons miraculously found themselves outside of Communist-controlled territory.

This situation did not last long. The Soviets fooled the Germans into thinking that Lithuania would be a joint sphere of influence, but in fact, as soon as the Lithuanians reentered the "freed territories," the Soviets began to encourage local Communist elements. Two months after the yeshiva arrived in Vilna, the government of Lithuania ordered the refugees to disperse into the nearby townships. Eventually, the authorities agreed to allow the yeshiva to settle in the city of Kaidan, which was "deep" inside Lithuania, between Kovna and Ponivez. Lithuania's small area, however, meant that all parts of it were relatively close to the border. The symbol of the State of Lithuania was a rider on a horse standing on its two hind legs, its front hooves up in the air. The widespread joke was that if the horse would stand with all four of its legs on the ground, it would find itself standing in a neighboring country.

In Kaidan, a local committee was established to find a suitable location for the yeshiva and its dormitory. There the yeshiva spent eight months, during which extraordinary efforts were made to obtain exit visas from the war area with no success. The Communist influence in the country was growing stronger as the Russians slowly took over parts of Lithuania with the excuse that they were establishing bases for its defense. That summer, they established a Communist government in "Free Lithuania," and about two weeks before they finally annexed Lithuania, the Communists ordered the yeshiva in Kaidan closed.

In a country as small as Lithuania, it was impossible to covertly keep the yeshiva intact. Hundreds of *bochurim* and all that was necessary for their spiritual and physical survival made it too noticeable a body. The yeshiva directorate decided to divide the yeshiva into four groups. Quickly, four small towns close to Kaidan were chosen—Krak, Krakinova, Shat, and Ramigolah—and arrangements were made for the *bochurim* to move. The yeshiva's main center was Krakinova. Rav Laizer Yudel ostensibly cut off all contact with the yeshiva and worked underground from the town of Grinkishok, which was close to Kaidan. Student organizers came and went from there secretly, trying to obtain exit visas and involving themselves in all the yeshiva's activities.

Throughout its wanderings, from the time the Russians entered Mir until the yeshiva dropped anchor in Japan, it actually benefited from political and territorial upheavals. Roving from place to place allowed it relative quiet. As long as the invading army was new to a place and still organizing itself, its activities were relatively restrained.

When Lithuania was annexed, intensive efforts were made to get the yeshiva out. This is not the place to relate the details of the miraculous way in which the *hashgachah* arranged the yeshiva's salvation. One thing, however, can definitely be said: the obtaining of exit visas and the whole complex of strange events that surrounded it was a dimension of creation *yesh me'ayin*.

The wanderings, the hunger, the tumult of the refugees, the constant changes of government, the rumors that began to pour in from the war area, and above all, the constant feeling of being in a closed trap did not affect the spirit of the yeshiva. An entire year of Torah study in an atmosphere of terror and despair did not dishearten or distract the *talmidim*. The *mashgiach*, the Gaon and Tzaddik Rav Yechezkel Levinstein, continued to give inspiring *shmuessen* which breathed new life into anguished hearts. Rav Chaim continued to deliver regular *shiurim*, and the yeshiva was carried forward on waves of *hasmadah*, deep learning, and spiritual progress as never before. During this entire period, Rav Chaim did not alter his habits in any way. He continued learning with a *chavrusa* and started a new cycle of *shiurim*, which were far superior to any he had ever given.

All efforts on behalf of the yeshiva, many of which Rav Chaim was personally involved in, were carried out in ways and at times that did not interfere with the *sedarim*. The *chavrusos* who learned with him at that time and had previously learned with him in the Mir recall that he was at his best, and their feeling of spiritual improvement was stronger than in the Mir in Poland.

After the Kaidan period, once the yeshiva had split into groups, the directorate still made every effort to maintain a spirit of unity. The *mashgiach* would regularly trudge from one town to another to lighten the spirits of the *talmidim* with his stimulating *shmuessen*. He elaborated the principle that the *hashgachah* of turmoil and the events that develop from it are an act of kindness. Rav Chaim also circulated among the different groups, and his strong spirit did much to inspire the love for and devotion to Torah that distinguished that critical period.

Rav Chaim's powers of observation and reflection were brought to bear on the spiritual significance of the unfolding events. He associated detail with detail, event with event, and moral lesson with moral lesson to draw a highly meaningful picture. He saw the period as an open book. Only a man of his stature could articulate from the perspective of *Chazal* the spiritual and ethical lessons for both individual and community to be derived from such events.

One of the lessons that he often discussed in later years was *maalos haklal*, the advantage of being part of a community.

" 'Man ate the bread of the mighty.' This refers to Yehoshua, for whom manna fell down as it did for all of Israel" [*Yoma* 75b].

Is it talking about quantity? If it is, why did Yehoshua need so much manna—the same quantity as all of Israel?

It must mean something else. Yehoshua accompanied Moshe to the bottom of the mountain. He wanted to cleave to his rebbe another few minutes before Moshe ascended the mountain and meet him as soon as he descended. How far was it from the bottom of the mountain to the Israelite camp? From the bottom of the mountain, Yehoshua could hear what was going on in the camp! How far was Yehoshua from the camp? A walking distance of a few minutes, perhaps half an hour.

The manna descended for *Klal Yisroel*. At the bottom of the mountain, there is no manna. The manna descends because of the merits of the community; the individual receives his portion through the merits of the entire community. When one distances oneself from the community, even a little, a walking distance of only fifteen minutes, he needs personal merits equivalent to the merits of the entire community to receive sustenance and avoid starvation.

It is obvious that a collection of individuals doesn't make a community. The collection of individuals that makes up a community has to be of one mind—one person, one unit. Where such a community has been created, each individual who is a part of the community merits, and if, heaven forbid, he distances himself, then, heaven forbid, he sacrifices his life!

We have seen this with our own eyes. During the wanderings of the Mir, those who remained with the yeshiva were not harassed—all of them got out safely from the terrible exile—but those who segregated themselves even slightly—those who just went to say goodbye to their families in nearby towns, intending to return immediately—never returned.

The concept of the unity of the yeshiva guided all the decisions that were made in six years of exile, in Europe, Japan, and China.

*   *   *

The Gaon Rav Laizer Yudel Finkel was miraculously included in a group who received exit visas to emigrate directly from Lithuania to Eretz Yisroel. He took leave of the yeshiva, handing the leadership over to his son-in-law, Rav Chaim.

When the yeshiva finally received exit visas to Japan, it first had to travel by train to the port of Vladivostok. During the entire eleven day journey from Moscow to Vladivostok, Rav Chaim learned continuously with a *chavrusa*. One of the group that traveled with him on the ship from Russia to Japan relates that he did not talk about any subject other than Torah.

Rav Chaim once expressed the intense feelings he felt on departing from the Communist yoke. He said in his *shmuessen* that there are moments in life when a person is immersed in a deep awareness and readiness to accept a certain spiritual responsibility.

The mitzvah of freeing slaves came into effect only after Eretz Yisroel was conquered and the land divided among the tribes, but the first commandment concerning this subject was made on the day of the exodus from Egypt: "I made a covenant with your fathers on the day that I brought them forth out of the land of Egypt, out of the house of bondage, saying, 'At the end of seven years you shall send away your brother the Hebrew who has been sold to you. When he has served you six years you shall let him go free'" [*Yirmiyahu* 34:13]. Why was the commandment given then? After all, it would not be put into practice for many, many years.

There are moments in life a person remembers very well. These are the moments whose significance he experiences with maximum awareness. These are the times to accept *kabbolos*. Only if a person is well aware of the significance of an undertaking will he remember it and fulfill it. The day of the exodus from Egypt was the day on which the Jewish people became aware of the concept of freedom from servitude. There was no more fitting day to receive the commandment concerning the freeing of slaves.

I have had many great moments in my life, some more joyful, some less. Some of these moments are impossible to forget. When we sailed from the port of Vladivostok, from Russia, we were not convinced that the moment of freedom had come. Russian warships escorted us until we left their territorial waters. Russian officials accompanied us on our ship. We sat silently, afraid to express our joy lest it rebound on us—maybe they would change their minds. When we left Russian waters, these officials left our ship, and the warships steamed away. When we realized the significance of this parting, in one split second everything became lighter. A great song burst forth from our throats, and our feet danced, as if by themselves. A tremendous joy filled our hearts. I have had my moments...but that moment I will never forget.

Group by group, the *talmidim* of the Mir Yeshiva arrived at the Japanese port of Saroga, from where they traveled by train to the harbor city of Kobe. One of the *talmidim* had arrived earlier. He was waiting at the train station to welcome Rav Chaim. Rav Chaim stepped off the train, and, before the *talmid* could greet him, exclaimed, "Oh! Now we can sit and learn like the good old times."

Twenty years before the outbreak of the war, *hashgachah* had arranged for a few Russian-Jewish families to settle in Kobe. That community of about twenty-five families knew in advance that the yeshiva was arriving and arranged suitable accommodations. Representatives of the community welcomed the yeshiva warmly. Most of them were people of means, and they continued to support the yeshiva even after the American Jewish aid societies started sending financial support.

Once the yeshiva settled in Japan, regular *sedarim* resumed. A few *seforim* had been brought along, and the president of the yeshiva in America, Rav Avrohom Kalmanowitz, arranged for a shipment of two hundred copies of *Kiddushin*. A building on a high hill overlooking the scenic harbor was rented, and once again the voice of Torah was heard from the Mir Yeshiva with incomparable diligence and fervor.

Their stay in Japan was illegal, however; they had been given transit visas valid for only ten days. These visas had been issued on the basis of a special permit (attained in a miraculous way) which stated that they had final visas to the island of Curacao, which was under Dutch rule. The Japanese authorities placed many obstacles in the way of the yeshiva, making their stay in Japan uncomfortable. From time to time, the Japanese agreed to lengthen the temporary transit visas in return for repeated promises that every effort was being made to obtain entry visas to a different country.

The Americans were still issuing entry visas to small groups or to individual refugees who wished to emigrate there, but the principle that guided the yeshiva administration was unequivocal—either the entire yeshiva or no one at all. The tremendous pressure exerted on the American government was to no avail. There was no way to bring the entire yeshiva there. Eventually, the American Committee of the yeshiva obtained an entry visa for Rav Chaim; it hoped that he would spearhead the efforts that many different organizations were making to put pressure on the American administration. Rav Chaim replied with complete resolve that he would not leave the yeshiva for even one hour. The attempts of the American committee to obtain visas for at least a small group of *talmidim* were dismissed by Rav Chaim. The yeshiva was not to be divided! Even the threat by the Japanese consul that he would impound and revoke Rav Chaim's transit visa if he did not leave for America was of no avail. "I am prepared to travel to America only if it is with the entire yeshiva," he wrote in reply to those who were trying to convince him to leave. The result of this deep awareness that the yeshiva had to remain united at all costs was that even individual *talmidim* who did receive entry visas to the United States did not use them. Finally America closed its doors to all Jewish war refugees.

The tolerant atmosphere in Japan slowly deteriorated. Nazi Germany tightened its connections with Japan and "warned" the Japanese about the "dangerous Jews" living in their midst. A plan to spread defamatory literature about the Jews living in Japan was foiled with the help of Professor Kotsuji, a member of the Japanese royal family. Because of his interest in Semitic languages, he had come from Tokyo to gain first-hand knowledge of Hebrew and Aramaic. His good efforts were instrumental in arranging the repeated renewal of the transit visas, but when the Nazi influence on the Japanese royal family increased, he had to flee. He eventually converted to Judaism, adopting the name Avrohom Ben Avrohom.

The *talmidim* of the Mir Yeshiva were joined by hundreds of *talmidim* from other *yeshivos, roshei yeshiva, gedolei Torah, rabbonim*, and other refugees. A group of some two thousand people was stuck in Japan. Finally, the closing of all emigration points brought efforts to gain entry visas to other countries to an end. The Japanese then ordered all the refugees to move to the Chinese city of Shanghai which was under Japanese rule.

The Chinese had divided Shanghai into different sectors which housed the communities of different Western countries. They had given semi-administrative autonomy to these communities, and after the Japanese invasion, this system continued. The order to move there, however, caused depression to spread through the yeshiva. The city was at "the end of the world." Originally a place of exile for undesirables from many countries, the city had a motley refugee population and a busy harbor, with all the negative characteristics that such cities have. The yeshiva directorate, however, perceived the order to move in a different light. They assumed that the Japanese did not want to have a large group of undesirables within their borders and had therefore decided to transfer them to Shang-hai so that their illegal stay would not be so noticeable. Although Shanghai was also under Japanese rule, it appeared that their stay there would be under more tolerable conditions, which they desperately needed. The fact that the Japanese were willing to allow the entire yeshiva to transfer to Shanghai meant that it could continue to function. The month of Elul was approaching, and it was imperative to create a settled atmosphere, one that would be free from threats of further decrees and daily upheavals and doubts. These thoughts induced the yeshiva directorate to acquiesce without delay to the order of the authorities, and toward the end of the summer recess of 1941, the Jewish refugees in Japan moved to Shanghai.

Once the yeshiva arrived in Shanghai, its leaders briefly renewed their efforts to obtain entry visas to America. Then the Japanese bombardment of Pearl Harbor opened a new chapter in the war. America now became an enemy country, and any contact with it was considered treachery and spying. All efforts to obtain entry visas to America had to cease.

Three months after the beginning of the Shanghai exile, the Japanese started to deal more harshly with Shanghai, and refugees living in the city began to suffer the rule of a new type of oppressor, one who received his inspiration for anti-Semitism from his Nazi allies. Direct contact with yeshiva supporters outside of Japan was severed, postal and tele-graphic services ceased, and the refugees found themselves cut off from the outside world and under the constant surveillance of the Japanese secret police.

*   *   *

The Mir was situated in the Beis Aharon Synagogue in Shanghai's international sector. The story of the building of this spacious and beautiful synagogue in an area where Jews had never lived, and its availability to house the yeshiva, is yet another link in the long and amazing chain of events in which even the spiritually blind cannot help but see the hand of *Hashem*.

Rav Chaim's first *shiur* in Shanghai, on Rosh Chodesh Elul, 1941, opened one of the most glorious periods in the history of the Mir. From the time it arrived in Japan, a large number of affiliates of other *yeshivos* came under its wings, their connections with their own *yeshivos* having been cut off. Naturally, they gravitated toward the one organized body that still retained the original format of the old *yeshivos* of Lithuania and Poland. All looked to Rav Chaim, who demonstrated great resourcefulness and an unlimited willingness to assume responsibility whenever necessary. Approximately four hundred *bochurim* were totally reliant on him. This demanded self-sacrifice, leadership, audacity, and an awareness of the practical means to ensure material survival, which even in normal times were difficult and complicated. Everyone was amazed. What experience did Rav Chaim have with the practicalities of life—with a cruel world of plots and conspiracies—with anything other than *sevaros*? What chance did an inexperienced captain have amidst the dangerous icebergs that threatened to smash to pieces the ship of Mir at any moment? For years Rav Chaim had left people with the strong impression that he knew nothing of what was going on around him. (There were those who testified that in Mir he had no idea what a coin looked like.) Seemingly against all logic, an unknown side of his amazing personality now revealed itself. In his opinion, the weight of responsibility that rested on his shoulders left him no choice but to succeed. "An irresponsible person is a fool. Responsibility is the foundation of a human being," he used to say.

In later years, he would speak about two fundamental *mussar* principles which he combined to explain human capability in times of stress and necessity.

The strengths that lie within a human being are not always those that one can see in daily life. Within him are unimaginable resources. *Chazal* relate that Rav Amram Chassida managed to move a ladder that could normally only be moved by ten people [*Kiddushin* 31b]. How was this possible? When he saw that he was about to sin, he shouted in a loud voice, "There is a fire in Amram's house!" The Maharsha explains that he did not lie, heaven forbid. There was a fire burning within him. Life shows us that when a fire breaks out, a person tries to save whatever he possibly can and reveals superhuman strength. New strength, you think. No! No! This is the true, the real person. He just has to feel the heat of the fire....

The Rogatchover Gaon said of Rav Meir Simcha that he was a physically weak person, but when he saw the world aflame he was filled with unbelievable strength. Which strength? His own strength!

It is said about Yaacov, "And he lay down to sleep there." *Chazal* tell us that "there" he lay down to sleep, but the entire fourteen years he studied in the yeshiva of Ever, he did not lay down to sleep. How is this possible? The Gemara [*Nedarim* 15a] states, "If one says, 'I swear not to sleep for three days,' he is whipped [because it is impossible to stay awake for three consecutive days], and he may sleep immediately. So how is it possible that Yaacov did not sleep for fourteen years? The explanation is simple. Yaacov knew he was going to Lavan's house, and in Lavan's house a fire burned. When a fire is burning, everything is possible!

Moshe Rabbenu complains to *Hashem*, "Why are you treating me so badly...don't you like me anymore? Why do you place such a burden upon me? Was I the woman who was pregnant with this nation? Did I give birth to them? But you told me that I must carry them in my bosom as a nurse carries an infant....Where can I get enough meat for all these people? They are whining to me to give them meat to eat" [*Bamidbar* 11:12]. A heavy load—a very heavy load—and Moshe's question is a good one: where can I get enough meat for all these people?

Do you know who is allowed to ask such a question? The person who can ask, "Was I the woman who was pregnant with this nation? Did I give birth to them?" A father doesn't ask such a question. A father takes responsibility for his children. Even if he has six hundred thousand children, he cannot ask "Where can I get enough meat?" Where? A father has means. He who takes responsibility doesn't ask questions.

Rav Chaim acted according to his principles of responsibility. His personality was a synthesis of two seemingly contradictory characters, the loving father and the forceful leader.

Yakum of Zeroros was the nephew of Rav Yossi ben Yoezer of Zeredah. Riding on a horse, he passed the beam on which Rav Yossi was to be hanged, and taunted him: "See the horse on which my master has let me ride and the horse upon which your master has made you ride." "If it is thus with those who anger Him, how much more so with those who do His will," Rav Yossi replied. "Has then any man done His will more than you?" asked Yakum. "If it is thus with those who do His will how much more so with those who anger Him," Rav Yossi retorted. This pierced Yakum like the poison of a snake, and he went and subjected himself to the four modes of execution inflicted by *beis din*....Yossi ben Yoezer fell into a doze and saw Yakum's bier flying in the air. "By a little while Yakum has preceded me into the Garden of Eden," Rav Yossi said.

(Midrash Rabbah, Bereshis 65:22)

Look at what *Chazal* teach us about great people. He knew he was about to be hanged, and *Chazal* tell us that he "dozed"! Just see what a human being is capable of. Such calmness! From where does it come?

(Rav Chaim Shmulevitz)

SIX

IN THE EYE OF THE STORM

RAV CHAIM was the yeshiva's official representative to the authorities, so the Japanese secret police concentrated their attention on him. He was officially responsible for any failure by the *bochurim* to follow rules and for all deviations from official regulations. It was up to Rav Chaim to find a reasonable and acceptable explanation for how hundreds of *bochurim*, who were not working, had the means to survive. It was obvious to the Japanese that the yeshiva was financed from abroad, but it was imperative that they never find out that it was receiving "traitorous" American money. In fact, the yeshiva's American committee and the American Jewish refugee aid associations were its only sources of support. One has to bear in mind that millions of dollars were involved, which was equivalent to billions in local currency. A system for bringing such large funds into Japan had to be devised for wartime conditions of virtually no communication with the outside world, and the apparatus had to be assembled from scratch.

Through brilliant stratagems, a communications network with the outside world was established. Ostensibly innocent and perfectly harmless, these communications comprised a clever, sophisticated code system. Created by Rav Chaim, this code was based on halachic definitions, hints at subsections in *Shulchan Aruch*, numerology, and pseudonyms. Telegrams and letters, whose contents would appear completely innocuous to the secret police, were sent to neutral countries from the central post office in Shanghai. The secret police could be counted on to examine each word carefully, and they often demanded explanations. At first, the recipients of the letters found them difficult to decode, but once they had grasped the system, decoding became simple. The most complicated issues, including possible means of escape from the Japanese, were discussed in these letters and telegrams. They were understood by both sides as if an open discussion were taking place. The channels of communication operated via Uruguay, Sweden, and Switzerland.

The cornerstone of the system that supplied the yeshiva with money was a secret fund of dollars held by the Shanghai branch of an American bank. The Shanghai branch could not disburse money to the yeshiva unless it received an acknowledgment from the central bank in America that an equivalent sum of money had been deposited there. But no acknowledgment could exist in black and white. Rav Chaim would present the bank with an acknowledgment written in code. At first the bank in Shanghai refused to accept Rav Chaim's strange talmudic explanation of the coded message as the basis on which to issue large sums of money. Rav Chaim was faced with a problem: the money had been deposited in America, an acknowledgment of this deposit had been received in Shanghai, but the Shanghai bank was not convinced that his explanation of the acknowledgment was correct. He suggested that the dispute be settled by a court of arbitration consisting of three parties, one to be chosen by the bank, one by the yeshiva, and the third to be agreed upon by both. The bank agreed, and, finally, the court was convinced by Rav Chaim that the coded acknowledgments were honest and acceptable.

The complicated secret network, which had to be maintained to ensure the flow of money, would have done credit to a long-established organization. Some idea of the difficulties involved can be gained from the fact that even an experienced and efficient organization like the Joint Distribution Committee was unable to communicate with Shanghai: funding earmarked for refugees from the "Joint" had to come in the form of loans from members of the local Shanghai community.

The whole system established by the Mir was dependent on one man—Rav Chaim. He tried his best not to be involved in any other activities and single-handedly carried the entire responsibility. In constant danger, he put his trust in *Hashem*. Not only did Rav Chaim endanger himself for the yeshiva, but even for *bochurim* who had never crossed the yeshiva's threshold and had no connection with it. He would send telegrams on their behalf to their friends and relatives in faraway lands, and he, in fact, was the only individual in the refugee community who dared to and, indeed, succeeded in making contact with the outside world. When money for a *bochur* arrived, the joy he felt was indescribable, even though its receipt constituted a real danger for him: all such payments were in "illegal" United States dollars, checks and the like, and they were always made out to him personally.

Rav Chaim was constantly waging a war of minds with the cruel and sly Japanese secret police. The smallest slip could have landed him before a firing squad or in a Japanese prison, where, it was said, the cells were sprayed with deadly germs.

The latter was not just an unfounded rumor. At one point, seven Jews died in prison. The refugees decided to do post-mortem examinations on their bodies to determine the cause of their deaths and publicize in some manner the cruel acts of the degenerate Japanese. The secret police would not allow any postmortems. The bodies were handed over to the Jewish community immediately before burial, and during the funeral, secret police agents watched to make sure that the bodies were not spirited away. The agents remained on the scene until the bodies were buried.

The very mention of the "gendarmerie"—the secret police—made the spine shiver and the legs shake. Everyone's prayer was that he should never be connected with any event that might interest the secret police. Rav Chaim, however, stood at the head of the largest organized Jewish body in Shanghai, and this was, in itself, enough to make him a subject of prime interest. He was often called to police headquarters to "answer questions." The all-powerful Japanese official in Shanghai—Ghoya was his name—was cruel and slippery, and did not hide his feelings or intentions. Each time he went for an interrogation, Rav Chaim would say *viduy* and pray to *Hashem* that his words (and his legs) would not fail him. "A time of danger is the ideal time for prayer," he used to say. On one occasion, when it seemed that the secret police did have incriminating evidence against him, he raised his eyes to heaven and exclaimed, *"Ribono Shel Olam,* I was not born a yeshiva administrator *(menahel),* and I don't want to die one!" At his third daughter's wedding, Rav Chaim told the following story:

I was called to the headquarters of the Japanese secret police in Shanghai....I knew what they wanted to know....On what are three hundred and fifty non-

working yeshiva *bochurim* living? Everyone knew no
one returned alive from the third floor of the secret
police headquarters. A deathly fear fell upon me as I
walked up the stairs, and, as I walked, I prayed. Listen
to what I said: "*Ribono Shel Olam,* if you have chosen
me as a sacrifice, I am joyfully willing to be one. But if
I return alive, *Ribono Shel Olam,* I ask of you three
things." I had the right to ask, for Rava says when a
human being is in fear of death, he is permitted to make
requests from God—and I requested three things. I said
to *Hashem,* "The first thing I request from you, *Ribono
Shel Olam,* is that when I am deserving of release from
this *gehinnom,* you free me from any financial responsibility for the yeshiva. Also, *Ribono Shel Olam,* may my
daughters marry *talmidei chachomim.* Third, I ask,
Ribono Shel Olam, that I should merit sons who are
talmidei chachomim." This is what I said to God when
I went up those stairs. If the only consequence of the
whole episode was my fear of death, so be it, for when
one is in fear of death, one may make requests from
God. I can't tell you what happened up there on the
third floor, but I returned. Two of my prayers have
already been fulfilled. I am freed from financial responsibility for the yeshiva, and my third daughter is now
marrying a *talmid chacham.* With the help of God, my
third prayer will also be fulfilled!

At one stage, the Japanese ordered the yeshiva *bochurim* to
wear identification tags on their lapels. They were also ordered
to carry at all times special passes to cross from the Hongkew
sector (which later became the Jewish ghetto) to the international sector, where the Beis Aharon synagogue was situated.
These passes indicated the name of the bearer, the community

to which he belonged, where he was coming from, and his destination. He was not permitted to travel any further than the destination on the pass. It also recorded the times when it was permitted for the bearer to travel from the point of departure to his destination. Along the roads, there were open and concealed checkpoints where these passes were scrutinized.

When they traveled in groups, the *bochurim* didn't have problems. When a *bochur* traveled alone, problems arose. On Shabbos, they refrained from wearing their identity tags and carrying their passes, and crossed secretly from one sector to another. Inevitably, some were caught. Any time one of the *bochurim* was arrested for contravening a government or police order, it was Rav Chaim's responsibility, as the yeshiva's recognized official representative, to arrange for his release. Attempting the release of a *bochur* was like entering a lion's cage. The slyness and cruelty of the Japanese knew no limits, and one could never predict in advance the outcome.

One night the police raided Rav Chaim's house and found that the *chavrusa* he was learning with was outside the boundaries of Hongkew during illegal hours. Rav Chaim and his *talmid* were arrested with two other *bochurim* suspected of similar "crimes." Although this was not a serious crime, there was little doubt that the Japanese would search Rav Chaim's house and easily find a hidden hoard of American dollars. The danger of death hovered over Rav Chaim's head. Those arrested were aware of the danger, and they waited fearfully to see what would happen. The situation appeared desperate, yet Rav Chaim's attitude was one of complete nonchalance. Amid the tumult raised by the drunks and criminals around him, he stood the entire night by the bars of the large cell looking out onto the corridor. As he stood there, he silently reviewed a difficult *sugya* in *Mesechta Shabbos.*

The next day a miracle took place. At the time of his arrest, no police agents had been free to search his house. The following morning a *bochur* from another yeshiva, who had also been arrested and was being interrogated, overheard the name of Rav Chaim being whispered by secret police agents. He managed somehow to get a message out to Rav Chaim's wife, who did not know what had happened to him. She took the hoard of dollars and hid it in a neighbor's house. When the secret police finally searched the house, they found nothing. Rav Chaim and his *chavrusa* were brought to trial, and he was sentenced to three days imprisonment. He was released close to Shavuos. When he parted from the two *bochurim* who had to remain in jail, he encouraged them by telling them that the important thing to remember was not to abandon one another. "Orpa stayed away from her mother-in-law, and look what happened to her. Ruth cleaved to her mother-in-law, and see what she merited!"

*　　　*　　　*

For the yeshiva's *talmidim,* the lack of any connection with the outside world—with neither friends nor relatives—was both depressing and oppressive. The enforced solitude in time of war, when every person is hungry for any crumb of information; the feeling of being lost in a strange land on the other side of the world, a land where piles of corpses were collected from the streets each morning; the feeling of besiegement under the yoke of a pro-Nazi government, which was seemingly sharpening its knives; the fears and rumors about what had happened to loved ones and relatives left behind in the raging fires of Europe; the lack of knowledge about what was happening today and what tomorrow held in store—all this, and more, weighed heavily on the yeshiva students and made their dependence on the yeshiva and its directorate almost total. The situation was aptly described by one of the alumni of Shanghai: four hundred *bochurim,* four hundred problems. The yeshiva was father, mother, family, and savior to each one of them.

There is no doubt that the relentless pursuit of learning and the frequent *bitachon*-saturated *shmuessen* of the *mashgiach* were an escape for the emotionally exhausted *bochurim.* Torah, *mussar, hasmadah,* and encouraging words all constituted a life-giving transfusion for depressed souls. It is interesting that in the hellhole of Shanghai, the yeshiva reached its all-time spiritual height. During this period, Rav Chaim constantly demanded from its students a deep awareness of God's open miracles, which the *hashgachah* was showing them at every step.

Nevertheless, the situation often created deep feelings of depression and bitterness, and, as might have been expected, the latter were often aimed at the individual on whom all depended—Rav Chaim. Indeed, some even felt that it was permissible to voice their opinions and reservations about the way the yeshiva's affairs were being run.

During the first winter after the war broke out, when all sources of financial support were abruptly cut off, and the new secret communications system had not yet developed flesh and bones, the yeshiva's financial situation was at an all-time low. It seemed that both its liquid assets and its stock of provisions would run out before Pesach. Anticipating this dire picture, Rav Chaim laid aside a large sum of money for Pesach expenses, and for some months, the yeshiva followed a policy of strict rationing.

Unconnected to this policy of rationing, most of the refugees suffered from "cracked tongues" from the time they arrived in Shanghai. This was a painful illness, whose symptoms were an oppressive dryness of the mouth and tongue, which resulted in the tongue's "cracking." Every drop of food caused a terrible burning sensation, and of course, this took its toll on everyone's learning. Medical experts in Shanghai expressed the opinion that the problem was caused by a lack of vitamin B, a deficiency that could lead to the more terrible disease of beriberi.

It is not difficult to imagine how those who were unfortunate enough to suffer from this illness felt. The severe rationing only added to their distress. There was much bitterness, and there were those who argued that "the present is most important." Rav Chaim obstinately withstood all these pressures with clear awareness that the entire responsibility for the yeshiva in these uncertain times rested solely on him. Eventually he was proven correct. The food supplies lasted until Pesach, and money he had set aside allowed the yeshiva to celebrate the *Yom Tov* in comfort. After Pesach, the "funding system" begun to function, and the yeshiva's lot improved considerably. "How would we have survived the winter if I had listened to them?" asked Rav Chaim.

On many occasions during the exile in Shanghai, when bitterness swelled up and expressed itself in loud voices, Rav Chaim would be forced to fend off his antagonists: "You are putting a family with small children into danger," he told them. Notwithstanding Rav Chaim's obstinacy, and the forceful way in which he defended his opinions against all challenges, he still listened to those whose opinions he respected. One of the "giants" among the *talmidim* of the yeshiva, the Gaon Rav Leib Mallin, once approached him with a different opinion. To everyone's surprise, Rav Chaim retreated from his position without hesitation—"Okay, we will do it the way you suggest." Because he demonstrated an unshakable ability to lead, the disciplined structure which unified the yeshiva was never threatened by collapse.

Rav Chaim had to tackle many complicated problems in addition to financial administration and establishing a firm,

authoritative framework. These often demanded improvisa-
tion, organizational skills, and the ability to make decisions.

Conditions in Shanghai, including the yeshiva's location,
were not stable. At first, the entire yeshiva was in the Beis
Aharon synagogue in the international sector. Later, the
learning center remained there, but the dormitory facilities
were moved to the Japanese Hongkew sector. After that, when
the Japanese started seriously considering the idea of anni-
hilating the Jewish population of Japan, the entire yeshiva
moved to the Japanese sector, which, in effect, became a Jewish
ghetto. Until the yeshiva was forced into the ghetto, the
mashgiach lived in the French and Rav Chaim lived in the
English sector. Any change in location or conditions threatened the spirit of learning in the yeshiva. Excellent organizational skills and practical common sense were needed to
minimalize any interference in the *sedarim*. Every move
necessitated a search for suitable dormitory accommodations,
and during the "ghetto" period the yeshiva was forced from
time to time to rent different buildings for use as a *beis
hamedrash*.

A single principle guided all yeshiva activities: not at the
expense of *sedarim*. The activists who helped the yeshiva
directorate with practical arrangements were in the main the
outstanding students.

One of the problems that plagued the yeshiva was its
limited library. The collection was made up of *seforim* brought
by the *talmidim* from Europe in their baggage, of the Gemaras
sent from America, and the few *seforim* in the Beis Aharon
synagogue. Some *seforim* were borrowed from members of the
Shanghai community. Many of the *seforim* were already torn
or tattered, and even those that were not did not remain whole
for long as they were passed continually from hand to hand.
One *bochur* had brought a single copy of *Ketzos HaChoshen*

from Mir, but it was missing two pages. Rav Chaim sat down and wrote out the missing pages from memory. Many years later, when his handwritten script was compared to the original, it was found that he had not missed one word! (The copy of the *Ketzos* with Rav Chaim's handwritten additions is still in the family's possession.) The serious shortage of *seforim* presented a problem that had to be solved, and the solution had to be local. The yeshiva established a publishing committee called *Torah Or*. During the years in Shanghai, *Torah Or* managed to publish a complete *Shass* with *Rif*, a number of *rishonim*, a *Rambam*, a *Shulchan Aruch*, and numerous works of *mussar*.

Under Rav Chaim's leadership, the yeshiva ran as if it belonged in Shanghai and would remain there forever. Even in the last year of its stay, when exit visas started to flow, the publishing committee continued its activities with drive and energy. No sense of impermanence was allowed to impede any of the many activities of the yeshiva. Nevertheless, the desire of every *bochur* to leave Shanghai as soon as possible, physically and spiritually in one piece, was an ongoing source of hope and encouragement. During the entire five years, efforts never ceased to find means to leave. A great number of coded telegrams were sent and received in connection with these efforts.

One of the worst problems in Shanghai was marriage. There were many refugees, especially German and Russian, whose religious standards were very low and whose daughters had reached marriageable age. There were also many older *bochurim* among the yeshiva's students who, if conditions had been normal, would have been long married. In spite of certain fears with regard to the religious standards of the daughters of these refugees, Rav Chaim encouraged the students to marry them. He would not treat the situation in Shanghai as temporary. "The power of Torah can burn everything," he argued.

In abject poverty, with the *talmidim* totally dependent on the yeshiva directorate and feeling like orphans, many material and spiritual obstacles had to be overcome to lead a couple under the *chupah*. Without Rav Chaim's help, this would have been impossible.

In spite of all the difficulties and obstacles, Rav Chaim worked like a faithful father to marry off the students. He and his wife, with the Rav of the Ashkenazic community of Shanghai, repeatedly served as *shushbinim* for the *chasan* and *kallah*. Once, as an honor and a *segulah*, a *kallah* wanted a childless couple to be *shushbinim*. The *chasan*, who wanted to give Rav Chaim this honor, objected strongly. When Rav Chaim heard about it, he tossed in bed the whole night. He understood the *kallah's* wishes and appreciated the *chasan's* feelings. In the morning, he sent a message to the *chasan* saying that he preferred that the childless couple be *shushbinim*. A year later, the childless couple gave birth to a son. More than twenty years later, Rav Chaim led the *chasan's* son under the *chupah*....Many glorious Torah homes were built from marriages that took place in Shanghai.

Rav Chaim's fatherly warmth expressed itself at weddings and other joyous occasions. It was on these occasions that he began to speak *divrei aggadah* for the first time in public. His wonderful reflections and brilliant explanations of different words of *Chazal* were the cause of much excitement. Those who remember his speeches from that period point out that the principles of *mussar* he discussed then were the very same principles that he continued to speak about to the end of his life. They just underwent greater elaboration and increased in depth.

Until the end of his life, he felt obliged to attend all the joyous events of his students and to console them in their times of sorrow. He was very particular to attend their

children's weddings, even when it meant getting up from his
sick bed in the hospital. When he heard of troubles, God forbid,
befalling a graduate of the yeshiva, he would tearfully daven
for him.

Many years after Shanghai, one of the Shanghai alumni
came to visit him in Eretz Yisroel. When Rav Chaim saw him,
he burst out crying, as if he had met a long-lost brother of
whom he had had no news. When the visitor prepared to
return home, Rav Chaim refused to bid him farewell until he
came to visit just once more. When he came to take leave of
Rav Chaim, as he had promised, Rav Chaim hired a taxi and
traveled with him to the homes of all his sons and daughters
throughout Jerusalem so they could also bid the visitor farewell. This all took place in the early hours of the morning.

Rav Chaim accepted the sons of Shanghai alumni into the
yeshiva in Jerusalem without hesitation. "They are members
of the family," he used to say. He used a warm expression for
his deep feelings of shared suffering on the voyage of the
troubled ship of Mir—"ship brothers." It expressed a deep
emotional attachment and complete willingness to sacrifice
and shoulder responsibility for others. A concrete expression
of his feeling that every individual from the refugee community in Shanghai was a "brother-in-destiny" surfaced at the
end of the war, when America opened its gates to refugees.
Rav Chaim personally petitioned for visas even for those who
had been far removed from the yeshiva circle.

He refused to accept an American visa for himself until the
last *bochur* in the yeshiva had received one. "I am the last in
turn of the *b'nei Torah*," he writes in one of his letters. Finally,
all the yeshiva students but one had received visas to America
or Canada. One of the *talmidim*, who had become mentally
disturbed, could not obtain a visa. The American immigration
authorities, sometimes lenient in cases of physical ailments,
were extremely particular about mental illness.

Rav Chaim let it be known that he had no intention of leaving the *bochur* behind in Shanghai. He came under heavy pressure to change his mind, and attempts were made, with the help of the local Jewish community, to find a suitable way to leave the *bochur* with the considerable number of other refugees who had not managed to obtain visas and who were being looked after by the local community. Rav Chaim remained firm: "The yeshivá will not travel without the *bochur*."

It was obvious to everyone that it would be impossible to get the *bochur* out of Shanghai by normal methods. One manifestation of his mental illness was his inability to give accurate information about his identity. Every day, he would present himself as someone else—this rabbi, that Chassidic rebbe, and so forth. A visa would have to be obtained in some roundabout way. The problem became more difficult when the *bochur* insisted on emigrating to Eretz Yisroel, something which was impossible to arrange at that time. He was willing to change his mind only after Rav Chaim promised him that if he traveled to America he, Rav Chaim, would try to get him appointed *rosh yeshiva!*

Rav Chaim's obstinacy concerning the *bochur* elicited many complaints. Any trickery that came to light would have spoiled the reputations of all the others who had received American visas and could even have resulted in the American authorities arbitrarily cancelling all visas. One day Rav Chaim walked into the yeshiva and revealed his response to this possible complication with the casual remark, "What would you do for a brother?"

He called together a number of students, including one who had some influence over the ill *bochur*, and they all went to the American immigration office. Earlier, Rav Chaim himself had taken the sick *bochur* to a doctor who had given a "recommendation" that his health was good. In the consulate,

Rav Chaim sat the *bochur* down next to him. While they were giving the official the information required, Rav Chaim was exerting strong restraint on him, but he suddenly sprang up from his chair and went wild. The hearts of those present stopped beating. Rav Chaim was in a precarious situation. He had been an active partner in an attempt to deceive consulate officials. Rav Chaim matter-of-factly turned to calm him down and sat him down in his place. Naturally, the official suspected that something was amiss. Rav Chaim casually explained that the *bochur* had been emotionally overwhelmed at the thought that the moment had arrived when his life's dream of emigrating to America was about to come true. The official accepted this and continued filling out the necessary details on the visa.

This, however, was only the first and "easy" stage. Every emigrant had to go into the consul's room, raise his hand, and declare allegiance to the American people and constitution. Considering the mental condition of the *bochur*, everyone once again had the feeling that a tragedy was about to take place.

A miracle happened. The woman who was acting as consul had to go somewhere in a hurry that afternoon. A long line of people were waiting outside her room. She came into the main hall, saw the crowd of busy officials and noisy applicants, and instructed all the applicants to raise their hands and declare their allegiance in unison. The disturbed *bochur* raised his hand. The consul quickly signed the visas of everyone present.

Rav Chaim, however, did not see this as the end of the story. He feared that the trick would be discovered on the long sea journey and the *bochur* denied entry to America. The only solution was to fly him to America, something rare in those days. Rav Chaim did not rest until he found a suitable flight. Taking into consideration the seriousness of the problem, he booked the flight despite the fact that it left on Shabbos.

On Shabbos morning, the *bochur* disappeared. Rav Chaim sent *bochurim* all over town to look for him. When he was finally found, Rav Chaim hired a taxi and ordered another *bochur* to accompany him to the airport to make sure he caught his plane.

With the kindness of God, the disturbed *bochur* completely recovered his health in America and established a wonderful family.

*   *   *

Nothing—no danger, no responsibility—could distract Rav Chaim from his exertions in Torah study. Under the most abnormal conditions, he continued to learn with *chavrusos* day and night, as in days gone by. With tremendous inner strength, he continued to say his *shiurim*, and although he was in his second cycle of saying *shiurim*, he did not make things easier for himself, but prepared entirely new ones. In Mir he had given a *shiur* only once a week—in Shanghai he gave a *shiur* twice a week. During the five years spent in Shanghai, Rav Chaim delivered four hundred *shiurim*. This *hasmadah* in the face of responsibility and danger was amazing. He had a tiny cubicle in the Beis Aharon synagogue, and there, behind a curtain, he sat and learned with a *chavrusa* without interruption. At night, he learned at home with a *chavrusa*.

His strong morale and efforts in Torah learning were a live torch that sent out sparks of *ahavas haTorah* and *dveikus ba'Hashem*. Toward the end of the war, when American planes were repeatedly bombing sectors of Shanghai, and the sound of the sirens sent shivers down each spine, when the houses of the Jewish ghetto were shaken again and again in bombing raids, he continued learning *Taharos* without interruption. His *ahavas haTorah* made no distinction between war and peace.

מוו״ר חיים סטוש
שליט״א

Rav Chaim Leib Stavisker

Rav Yeruchem Levovitz

Rav Yechezkel Levenstein

Rav Shimon Shkop.

Rav Eliezer Yehudah Finkel

Rav Chaim Ozer Grodzenski

Japanese transit visa

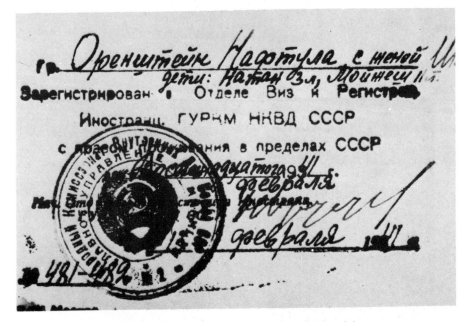

Soviet exit visa which had to be obtained by
refugees before they could leave Lithuania

HaGaon Rav Avraham Kalmanowitz

Telegram from Rav E.Y. Finkel to Rav Kalmanowitz

Letter from British Foreign Secretary Lord Halifax to Rabbi Avraham Kalmanowitz about Mir students in Shanghai

A group of refugees arriving in Japan

Mir Yeshiva student moving to Hongkew ghetto in Spring, 1943

Mir Yeshiva students in Kobe

Mir Yeshiva student in Lane 599, Tongshan Road

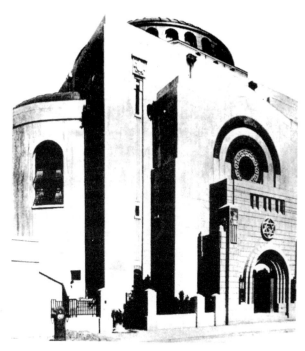

Beis Aharon Synagogue on Museum Road

Shanghai ghetto identification
badge

Ghoya

Professor Avraham Kotsuji and his grave in Jerusalem

Reception in the Mir Yeshiva, Jerusalem for Professor Avraham Kotsuji

Mir Yeshiva *beis hamedrash* in Beis Aharon Synagogue. Rav Chaim Shmulevitz is second from the right front.

Courtesy of Rabbi Dovid Movshovitz

משנה תורה

הוא

יד החזקה

להנשר הגדול רבינו משה בר מיימון זצ״ל.

עם השגות **הראב״ד** זצ״ל, וחידוש הרב המגיד **משנה**, דכסה **משנה** להגאון מרן יוסף קארו זצ״ל, **מגדל עז**, הגהות **מיימוניות** [עם תוספות מרמת״מ מיניציאל ס״י שרי״א], [עם הוספת הרב הגאון מהרי״ם פאדרוה זצ״ל], עם **תשובות מיימוניות**, וחידושי הרב רבינו **עובדיה** וחדב הגאון מהר״ל בן חביב על הלכות קדש החודש, עם כל הצורות החשיכות להם ולהלכות שבת וסוכה. עם **הלחם משנה** להגאון מ״ה אברהם די בוטן זצ״ל, **ומשנה למלך** להגאון מ״ה יהודה רוזאניס זצ״ל. כאשר היו בדפוס יעסניץ, דיהרנפורט, זיטק וברדיטשוב.

תלוה לז **ספר המקנ**ך חדושים ופסקי דינים מהרב הגאון ר' נהום טריביטש זצ״ל אבר״ק נ״ע כפי שנרשם בווין.

ועתה הוספנו חדשות אשר לא היו מעולם בכל ספרי הרמב״ם הנדפסים יראו נבונים וישמח:

א) פירוש דבמגיד **משנה** על הלכות שחיטה, אשר זה זמן כבתב יד ולא נדפס מסלם, נדפס על מקומו בפנים הספר.	יד) הסממבות מדמספה הטביר״ד, כראם מ״ה טמאל' שמראלן זצ״ל, וינזצא, שנת ש״י, סי״א.
ב) פירוש **הרדב״ז** על ספר קדש, הפלאה, זרעים, שמפטים, מסלא מסם דבמגיד **משנה** שלא נמצא בספרים האולה, נתל [מכ״י].	פו) חדושים ומקורים מהרב הגאון מ״ר אברהם זצ״ל אברלק פ״ש דסין, [מכ״י].
ג) חדושים ומקורים מהרב הגאון מ״ד זלמן זצ״ל מילעלא אור הגאול״נ מהר״ן זצ״ל מולהאון.	מז) חדושים ומקורים מהרב הגאון מ״ד מדור״ש ארדיעמסטין [נ״אברל״א אורקשא]וןל״א.
ד) חדושים ומקורים מהרב הגאון בעל פרי חדש, נקראים בשם מים חיים.	מז) חדושים ומקורים מהרב הגאון מ״ד משה נדוס נלזין ני' אברלק קאסלאנוא [מכ״י].
ה) חדושים ומקורים מהרב הגאון מ״ד מרב צבי הירש אפרים.	יח) חדושים ומקורים מהרב הגאון מ״ד צבי הירש הורוויץ זצ״ל.
ו) ביאורים על הלכות בית הבחירה מהרב הגאון ר' ישעיה פיק זצ״ל.	יט) באור בפרק י״ז, מקרוש החודש נתכנ מ״ר רפאל סלק הגובר זצ״ל.
	כ) עד כתינת שרח חים השרח, חאטי, פט שתי יחות לה״ג רם ד׳ מנואל זצ״ל.
ז) חדושים ומקורים מהרב הגאון מ״ד אברהם משכיל לאיתן זצ״ל, [מכ״י].	

פירוש דבמגיד **משנה**, והרדב״ז וזה בכתיבת יד. הגיעו לידינו פיד תהלק חמשה מהרל״ף ווסס אן י'ע ב״ץ זצ״ל אשר קה וזהם ברוך מרבית כתבי יד מעאות הראשונים, מאת רבני חכמי ספרד אשר בהדישם, שלמה להב בכסף סלא לך לצורך דבר מזוה נהלח, שנזעמרו או חדשטים באורתנג ד' ר' ה' יבאו בכסף כל ספר, וחדשים באוח ר' יבא בכסף ספר בדעה, הדשים מארת ר' ובעלה, כמף כל חלק סמי, חלקי הרמב״ז.

נדפס בהגהה, מריקת וטונקי מרבית הטעיות שנשתרבבו ברפומים הקודמים, כו בפנים הספר וכן בכל המפרשים מסביב.

נדפס בשנגהי

בהוצאת

ועד ההדפסה

״תורה-אור״

בשנת תשג יצק

Title page of Rambam's *Mishneh Torah*, published by the Mir Yeshiva in Shanghai

Rabbi Avraham Kalmanowitz thanking Henry Morgenthau Jr. for assistance in rescue work

Mir Yeshiva in Poland

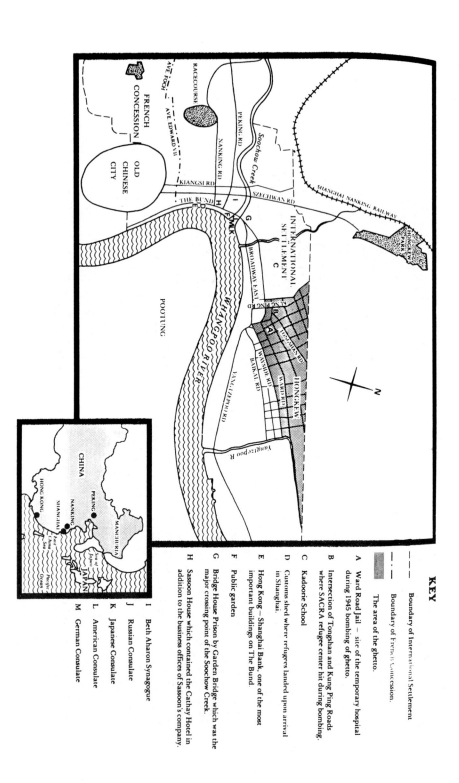

KEY

- - - - - Boundary of International Settlement

— · — · — Boundary of French Concession.

▨ The area of the ghetto.

A Ward Road Jail — site of the temporary hospital during 1945 bombing of ghetto.

B Intersection of Tongshan and Kung Ping Roads where SACRA refugee center hit during bombing.

C Kadoorie School

D Customs shed where refugees landed upon arrival in Shanghai.

E Hong Kong — Shanghai Bank, one of the most important buildings on The Bund.

F Public garden

G Bridge House Prison by Garden Bridge which was the major crossing point of the Soochow Creek.

H Sassoon House which contained the Cathay Hotel in addition to the business offices of Sassoon's company.

I Beth Aharon Synagogue

J Russian Consulate

K Japanese Consulate

L American Consulate

M German Consulate

Mir Yeshiva in Jerusalem

Mir Yeshiva in New York

Rav Chaim and Rav Mordechai Gifter

Rav Chaim and Rav Yitzchak Hutner

With superhuman power of concentration, he studied Torah as if the tumult going on around him did not exist.

The figure of Rav Chaim, his tireless exertion in Torah study and his obvious unceasing spiritual progress, served as a concrete example of the unlimited spiritual potential that exists in a human being under all conditions. He exemplified one of his own *mussar* principles about human potential: Man stores within him hidden strengths and powers that show themselves in times of catastrophe.

The history of Mir Yeshiva in Shanghai during the war is one of the most glorious pages in the history of *yeshivos*. During this period of war and great difficulties, the spirit of Torah and *mussar* reached heights that had never been achieved before in the yeshiva. The existence and progress of the Mir Yeshiva in Shanghai was a ray of hope in a dark, stormy sea of terrible destruction. Shanghai was a solitary island where the voice of Torah was heard loud and clear without interruption. There, the saplings were cultivated from which the academies of Torah destroyed in the terror of the Holocaust would be rebuilt.

*   *   *

The members of the Mir Yeshiva left Shanghai in groups on their way to the West Coast of America. A small group of *bochurim* who held American visas strongly desired to emigrate to Eretz Yisroel, but Rav Chaim preferred to travel with the main body of the yeshiva to America. His assumption was that in America, a bright future awaited the yeshiva. However, when his father-in-law expressed a preference that he emigrate to Eretz Yisroel, Rav Chaim immediately repressed his own feelings and joined those traveling there. This small group of *bochurim* who desired to go to Eretz Yisroel did not have entry certificates. They managed in a roundabout manner to obtain transit visas to France, using the argument that they wanted to enter America via New York. The French could hardly imagine that any rational person who held a valid visa for America would want to go to Palestine, where disturbing events were happening every day. They allowed the group to pass through France.

The journey by sea from Shanghai to France took four weeks. There were many hardships and delays, but these could not dampen the feelings of relief that accompanied this obvious miracle of salvation. Rav Chaim was not drawn into the general emotional state of the others. For the entire duration of the journey, he sat on the deck of the boat, holding on his lap the *Shev Shmaitzah,* which he studied diligently and eagerly. He wrote down *chiddushim* in a notebook he named *Toras Sephinah.* During those weeks, he filled it with thirty-two lengthy Torah essays.

On the ship's deck, everyone impatiently awaited the moment their feet would once again touch firm land. Rav Chaim, however, remained totally immersed in a difficult *sugya,* the effort of concentration apparent on his face. At one point, one of the *bochurim* who stood at his side gazing into the distance at a vast, empty expanse of water, asked aloud, "Where are we?" "The third chapter of *Shev Shmaitzah,*" answered Rav Chaim without hesitation.

Rav Chaim slept in a cabin with a priest who rose early every morning to pray. He tried to get up earlier than the priest. During the entire journey, when he was in the company of the priest, he continually repeated to himself the words of *Chazal:* "I get up early, and they get up early, I run and they run. I run to a life in the world to come and they..."

During the journey, the group made a number of illegal and unsuccessful attempts to disembark at different ports in order to get to Eretz Yisroel. Rav Chaim later related that, at that time, he was convinced that in Eretz Yisroel he would be able to learn twenty-four hours a day. Many dangerous efforts were made to disembark, but none were successful. Even the large sums of money they were willing to expend as bribes were of no avail. At one port of call, Rav Chaim's daughter was taken ill, and the ship was quarantined outside the harbor. The group found a way to smuggle itself ashore, but because of his daughter's illness, Rav Chaim was forced to stay on board. For an entire night, he helped his companions transfer their luggage to his cabin, so that he could, at a later date, send it to Eretz Yisroel. However, this attempt to disembark was also unsuccessful.

After they reached their destination, Marseille, he began an intense effort to obtain visas to Palestine. He traveled often to Paris to consult with aliyah officials and representatives of Jewish organizations, but to no avail. He was troubled by his long stay away from the yeshiva, an absence that seemed to have no purpose. Without the voice of Torah echoing around him, he found no peace. Just when he had decided to travel to America, from where, he had concluded, it would be easier to acquire the long-awaited certificate of entry to Eretz Yisroel, a possibility for his family to enter Eretz Yisroel opened up. The rest of the group, however, would have to wait more than a year until they could travel there, so Rav Chaim sent his family on to Eretz Yisroel and continued with the group to America.

His arrival in New York made a strong impression. Residents of the neighborhood in which he settled relate that people would stop in the street to gaze at his upright stature and shining face. His energetic walk and ramrod bearing gave him the quality of a young lion, and his unique reputation accompanied him everywhere and aroused great respect.

The entire yeshiva once again rallied around him. Many pleaded with him to reestablish the yeshiva; it was said that it could expect a brilliant future there. The few surviving products of the Lithuanian *yeshivos* were now to be found in America, and they were eagerly awaiting a teacher who could unify their ranks. The yeshiva held a great deal of interest for a wide cross-section of the Jewish community. This was obvious from the huge crowds that came to hear Rav Chaim's new and exciting *shiurim*, which he said in a style they were not at all used to. Yet it was clear to him that his days in New York were numbered. His family was already in Eretz Yisroel, and his father-in-law informed him that he wanted him there. He was being called to a yeshiva, headed by his father-in-law, which had only a handful of students. In America, he could have headed a yeshiva with hundreds of students. It would have been the largest yeshiva in the world, a true and faithful continuation of the prewar European *yeshivos*. But his obedience to his father-in-law, Rav Laizer Yudel, was total, and his departure for Eretz Yisroel was, therefore, only a question of time.

In conjunction with the yeshiva directorate in America, and without delay, Rav Chaim set about the task of reestablishing the yeshiva there. Once again, the question of a temporary stay did not constitute an obstacle. He toiled to get the yeshiva open and running on a normal schedule. Regular *shiurim* were arranged, a temporary building was found, and the voice of Torah was heard once again. Rav Chaim hoped that he could turn over his position to one of his star pupils before he emigrated to Eretz Yisroel. He soon realized that he was becoming heavily involved again in financial matters. In Shanghai, he had been forced to be actively involved in the monetary aspects of the yeshiva, but in America, he could refuse to do so, for there were others who were capable of worrying about finances.

Soon, Rav Chaim was able to bid farewell to his beloved students of the Mir Yeshiva and emigrate to Eretz Yisroel. Before leaving, he assembled a small elite group who would go with him to join his father-in-law's yeshiva in Jerusalem. There, this seed would sprout, opening a new chapter in the history of the Mir—*Mir d'Yerushalayim*, the Jerusalem Mir. With Rav Chaim's arrival in Eretz Yisroel, a saga of hardship, suffering, danger, and wandering came to an end.

*   *   *

An uninterrupted stream of letters came from America, begging Rav Chaim to return to head the yeshiva there. The ranks were falling apart; everyone saw him as the only one who had the strength and ability to take the initiative and pull it together. His refusal was unequivocal. From his short stay in New York, it had been clear to him that heading the American yeshiva would require involvement in so many activities that it would interfere with his learning.

With his arrival in Eretz Yisroel, he accepted his father-in-law's authority as *rosh yeshiva* in all matters, both spiritual and material. Difficult and bitter years of leadership and involvement in administration and decision making had left him without the slightest desire to remain in a role of authority.

During the period that he led the Mir in Shanghai, Rav Chaim had never considered himself its "owner." Rather, he had felt that he was entrusted with a valuable pledge for whose safety he was responsible, and he had behaved accordingly. Once that pledge had been safely returned, he had no further need for control or power. On the contrary, administrative duties were a contradiction to his very essence. To one of the longstanding Mir alumni, he once stated his clear opinion on the subject: "I would rather be a shoemaker than be involved in the financial administration of the yeshiva."

*   *   *

His father-in-law passed away in 1965. Rav Chaim's great respect and esteem for Rav Laizer Yudel, which had enabled him to so completely humble himself before him, was clearly expressed in the *hesped* he gave. He expressed in an unusual and concrete manner the feeling of mourning felt by the Torah world at the *petirah* of Rav Laizer Yudel.

If the Rebbe would walk in, what would we all do? In his honor we would all stand up! Now that he is no longer with us, in his honor, let us all sit on the ground.

Rav Chaim sat on the ground. The tens of thousands of participants in the funeral did not hesitate for a moment. As one man, all sat on the ground. It was a memorable and impressive expression of *kavod haTorah* and mourning. But no less than this, the event demonstrated Rav Chaim's powers of leadership and persuasion. His request was not met with hesitation—no one looked at his companion in confusion—rather, everyone followed Rav Chaim's example by sitting on the ground as if it was the most natural thing to do.

After Rav Laizer Yudel's death, the administration of the yeshiva was passed to one of his sons. Rav Chaim viewed this as a sign from heaven that his prayers in Shanghai had been accepted. He could now devote himself totally to the spiritual aspects of the yeshiva. Until his dying day, he was deeply grateful to his brother-in-law for relieving him of any financial involvement. At all family events and on every available occasion, Rav Chaim would publicize this kindness.

If a man leaves produce with his friend, even if it is deteriorating, the friend may not touch it. What is the reason? Said Rav Kahane: A man prefers a *kav* of his own to nine *kavim* of his neighbor.

(Bava Metzia 38a)

A *kav* of his own is dear to him because he toiled to produce it.

(Rashi)

But his desire is in the Torah of *Hashem*, and in his Torah he meditates day and night.

(Tehillim 1:2)

Initially it is described as "the Torah of *Hashem*," but after he has toiled in it, it is described as "*his* Torah."

(Rashi)

We are accustomed to thinking that *ahavas ha-Torah* leads to toil in Torah. Here we are told that toil in Torah leads to *ahavas haTorah*. See what an attachment to Torah toil leads to.

(Rav Chaim Shmulevitz)

SEVEN

A *KAV* OF HIS OWN

Y ERUSHALAYIM was an entirely different world. The outlook, methodology of learning, and, indeed, the human material were all very different from those of Eastern Europe.

Even though Rav Chaim initially lived and worked in Yerushalayim in the shadow of his father-in-law, he established a respected position very quickly among the ranks of the *b'nei Torah* community. Within a short time, he was famous in his own right. Standing on the *bimah* for his first public *shiur*, he looked like an aristocrat, very different from the rabbinic personalities in the city at that time. Word of his unique *shiurim* spread quickly, and people came from all over the city to enjoy his Torah.

He always wrote the sources for his *shiurim* on a piece of paper in six lines, each line always containing exactly the same number of words. The new generation, which knew little or nothing about the atmosphere of prewar Lithuanian *yeshivos*, slowly began to understand the uniqueness of his personality and realize that he was an extraordinary *gaon*.

Reminiscences from his *talmidim* stress three aspects of his personality in addition to his learning: simplicity and modesty, sensitivity, and a glorious blend of ideology and action, combining Torah, *mussar*, *yiras shomayim*, and mundane everyday activity.

He treated a *sevora* from any person with utmost seriousness and respect. Sometimes, when he heard a *sevora* from a young *bochur*, even a weak one, he would repeat it and review it again and again so as not to forget it. If he heard an incorrect *sevora*, however, he would react sharply. In the course of his learning with a *chavrusa*, he would often mention some *sevora* he had heard from a *bochur*, and sometimes even one he had heard from that *chavrusa*, who himself had forgotten the *sevora* long ago. Rav Chaim did not feel that it was degrading in any way to read Torah journals which contained *chiddushim* from young *bochurim*. He received tens of such journals in the mail. Often, while studying a particular *sugya*, he would remember a relevant essay in some journal and say, "Come, let us see what the young boy has to say." He maintained that the youngsters of our generation were generally superior in their *lamdonus* to the youngsters of previous generations: "Look at Torah essays in contemporary journals, and you will see that they are far superior to those published in previous years."

He encouraged the study of *acharonim*, and his own knowledge of them was mind-boggling: he could quote the latest *acharonim* verbatim. Although he mentioned dozens of them in his *shiurim*, he called the *Ketzos HaChoshen* "rebbe" and often said, "How can one move without him?"

Why should one originate *chiddushim* which have already been originated and published? This is like the genius inventor who locked himself in his laboratory and reappeared six months later to announce that he had invented electricity. You fool! If you are so brilliant and such a fruitful inventor, why do you waste your time and effort inventing that which has already been invented? Use existing inventions to invent something new.

He openly disdained authors who apologized to their readers in the introductions to their *seforim* for any *chiddushim* which might have already been published elsewhere. (These authors had not plagiarized *chiddushim*, but simply neglected to look into the works of other *acharonim*.) One such author, for instance, wrote in the introduction to one of his *seforim*, "It is not my method of learning to look into the works of the *acharonim*." In one essay, this author mentions a point debated by the Rashba in his responsa and concludes, "One must say that the Rashba made a mistake." Rav Chaim stood on the *bimah* completely enraged.

How can one say such a thing about the holy Rashba? The author has a question. The question has an answer. Where is the answer to be found? In the *acharonim*. The *Ketzos HaChoshen* asks the question and answers it. The *Nesivos* asks the question and answers it. And I, the insignificant, also ask the question and answer it. How can one write, on the basis of such a question, that a "mistake" was made by the holy Rashba? It is because the author was punished for not looking into *acharonim*.

*   *   *

When it came to *chavrusos*, Rav Chaim would learn with anyone who asked him, without taking into consideration the person's level. The *mesechta* or *sugya* to be learned would be determined after "taking advice" from his *chavrusa*. Once, when he was learning with two young *bochurim*, a third *bochur* asked to join in. "I must obtain permission from my *chavrusos*," Rav Chaim answered.

An elderly American rabbi, a graduate of the Stutchin Yeshiva, immigrated to Eretz Yisroel to pass the last years of his life there. Despite age and weak health, he asked Rav Chaim to study with him. Over a period of time, they managed to learn an entire *mesechta* together, until the old rabbi's health would no longer allow it.

Rav Chaim also had a *chavrusa* in one of the shuls in Yerushalayim, a man with a bedraggled appearance and strange mannerisms whose mental stability was in question. Once, an acquaintance couldn't restrain himself and asked Rav Chaim why he was learning with such a person. "What could I do? He asked me," Rav Chaim replied.

He learned differently with each *chavrusa*. With some he would analyze every word in the Gemara, *Rashi*, and *Tosafos*. He would read a line, half a line, or even only two words, and then repeat them ten, twenty, or thirty times. Then he would say, "Here 'so-and-so' comments," and taking a *sefer* from his bookcase, open it to the appropriate place and hand it to his *chavrusa*, asking, "What does he say?" The *chavrusa* had to look and explain the *sefer*. Rav Chaim would ask, answer, comment, or add, then say, "I think in 'such-and-such' a *sefer* there is an answer [or question, or comment]." Again, a *sefer* was brought to the table, opened, and the *chavrusa* had to explain, and so the cycle continued. His style of learning expressed a constant search for true understanding and demonstrated the necessity of accommodating all the particulars and finer points that make up the complete picture of the *sugya*. He investigated to the very roots of a *sugya*, suggesting different approaches and methods of clarification, defining, and again elaborating until everything became absolutely clear.

Before expanding on a subject, he would review aloud to himself points that required explanation, clarification, or further elaboration. He would present a simple translation of the words, explain them, then slowly list the questions pertinent to that particular point. So he would continue, until the subject became illuminated, clearly and simply. Rav Chaim called the result of this exercise *peshat*.

There are *b'nei Torah* who cannot distinguish between *poshut* and *peshat*. They believe that that which is *poshut*—which seems *poshut*—is in fact the *peshat*. This is a terrible mistake. There is *peshat* and there is *poshut*. Learning *peshat* is kosher learning. Learning *poshut* is *treif* learning.

Rav Chaim never tired of explaining a subject over and over until it was understood. At such times, he would sometimes cite other sources to make the subject more understandable. One of his *talmidim* remembers how Rav Chaim explained the concept of *havla'ah*.

There was an old woman who became ill. All she owned was a cow and a chicken. In her suffering, she made a vow that if God helped her and she recovered her health, she would give whatever she received for selling the cow to charity. God helped, and the woman recovered. The time now came to fulfill her vow. What did she do? She got up and announced that she would sell the cow for one dollar and the chicken for one hundred dollars, but she was not willing to sell one without the other!

He had dozens of such light and humorous parables. He used examples from everyday life to make subjects real, and would also invent stories with moral messages to illuminate the subject matter. He had a system of mnemonic devices, whose application could be so complicated that it was amazing he could remember the system itself, never mind the subject matter.

One of his *chavrusos* had difficulty absorbing all the material Rav Chaim covered with him in two hours. He asked Rav Chaim to write out the pertinent sources in shorthand so he could review. Rav Chaim gave him a long sheet of paper on which dozens of sources were listed. This preparation sheet and the others that Rav Chaim prepared regularly for a long time after reflected all the material to be discussed in the two hours of learning, except *chiddushim* that evolved during the actual *chavrusa*. The whole episode evoked awe and admiration in the *talmid*.

We use the expression *talmid*, but Rav Chaim was particular to use the word *chavrusa*. When someone came to visit, he would introduce the *talmid* with whom he was learning, with the words, "This is my *chavrusa*."

With some *talmidim*, he would learn a few lines each week, with others, entire *sedorim* of *Shass*. When they finished their first *mesechta*, Rav Chaim would divide the remaining time in halves, the first for review of the *mesechta* they had just finished, the second for learning the next *mesechta*. One year, he decided to learn *Nedarim*, *Gittin*, and *Kiddushin* with a *chavrusa*. Each time they finished a *mesechta*, they would review it in depth, making sure to cover all the different opinions of the commentators. He would systematically repeat the comments of all the *rishonim* and *acharonim* to the present day on every detail in the Gemara. He was very upset when this exercise took him a month longer than he had originally planned!

At different times, he had *chavrusos* to study *Ketzos, Nesivos, Shev Shmaitzah, Minchas Chinuch*, and other works. Even in his later years, his daily schedule commenced at five in the morning and finished at midnight or later. Each *chavrusa's* time was limited to either one and a half or two hours and not a minute more. When the time was up, Rav Chaim would stop and leave the *chavrusa*, even if they were in the middle of a subject.

He had eight or more *chavrusos* each day. The minute one left, another arrived. He studied a different topic with each one. Besides this, he presented a number of *chaburos* to *talmidim* of other *yeshivos*. Many groups requested *chaburos*, sometimes in *Kodoshim* and sometimes in *Taharos*. Once a group came to him with a request that he deliver *chaburos* on *Taharos* to them. "Okay," replied Rav Chaim, "in another twenty minutes, I'll say the first one." Twenty minutes later, the group gathered in his room, and Rav Chaim presented a *chaburah* which was so phenomenal in its depth and scope, it seemed as if he had been totally immersed in that particular subject for months. Along with his regular weekly *shiur*, Rav Chaim gave two *chaburos* a week to the *talmidim* of the Mir and three a week to *talmidim* from other *yeshivos*, all these in addition to his weekly *mussar shmuess* in the yeshiva *beis hamedrash*, the *vaadim* he gave, and the *shmuessen* he gave in his home on Friday nights and *motzo'ei* Shabbos.

Rav Chaim was always careful never to speak in public without preparation. Because he was considered so knowledgeable, his audience often lacked appreciation for the physical and spiritual toil he put into preparing his many *shiurim*.

It was difficult to fool him. He was totally aware of the audience's mood and their level of concentration and understanding. On many occasions, after presenting his initial series of questions, he would leave the room for a few moments to allow the participants time to digest them.

"Once, while he was delivering a *shiur*, Rebbe noticed the odor of garlic. He said, 'Whoever ate garlic should leave.' Rav Chiya rose and left....Rav Shimon, Rebbe's son, met him and asked, 'Was it you who annoyed my father yesterday?' 'Heaven forbid that such a thing should happen in Israel,' answered Rav Chiya. [Rav Chiya had acted with the intention of saving the real offender from humiliation.] And from whom did Rav Chiya learn such conduct?" [*Sanhedrin* 11a]

The Maharsha asks what difference does it make who Rav Chiya learned such conduct from? Who cares if he himself decided that this was the correct way to behave? The question is not a question. *Mesechta Avos* commences, "Moshe received the Torah from Sinai and transmitted it to Yehoshua." The Bartenura comments that this *mesechta* contains codes of ethical behavior. Therefore, it begins "Moshe received the Torah from Sinai" in order to teach us that these codes of ethical behavior were not created by the Sages, but originated from Sinai no less than the rest of the Torah. Torah without a proof and source is not Torah. The *chiddush* is that even normal human behavior—*middos*—need a source, for otherwise they are only man-made ethical codes. Now you know why the Gemara asks, "From whom did Rav Chiya learn such conduct?"

Rav Chaim made every effort to say new things in his *shiurim*, but as we have mentioned, he did not feel that every *chiddush* was suitable for the wider public. Time and time again he would review the subject matter with his *chavrusa*, look at his notebooks, and try to find a new approach for the *shiur*. At times he would go around in circles, finally arriving back at his starting point—the old *shiur*. He admitted that his encyclopedic knowledge sometimes did him a disservice. The sea of facts stored in his mind and the complexities of reconciling all these facts and making them clear and orderly took such a toll on his mind that he would exclaim, "My head can't absorb any more!" When he learned, he would pour out *chiddushim*, although sometimes he was forced to admit that these were *chiddushim* from previous years. He would often turn to his *chavrusa* and say, "Show your strength, make something new." *(Zy a berya, mach a nyer darher.)*

There was essentially no distinction, though, between "new" and "old." Those *shiurim* he had already given appeared in a new light when he repeated them. Even the ironic comments sounded as if they were being said for the first time. Rav Chaim's "knack" made the *shiur* sound as if it were new each time, and he imparted this feeling also to students who had heard the *shiur* a number of times already.

There was, however, no joy like his when he arrived at a novel approach to a *shiur*. He would literally lose himself in happiness. When *Pesachim* was included in the yeshiva curriculum, he studied that *mesechta* with his *chavrusa* from Purim until Shavuos and managed, in that short time, to originate thirty-two fundamental yet all-encompassing essays on *sugyos* in *Pesachim*, which he used as the basis for *shiurim*.

His *shiurim* in Yerushalayim, which were in the same style and encompassed the same wide field of knowledge as those he gave in Mir and Shanghai, were delivered with modesty and self-effacement. He would sometimes mention questions which had been asked in former years, even ones asked by younger students. Rav Chaim took all questions seriously, making every effort to avoid causing discomfort to the questioner by waving away his question in public or the like. He did not want to discourage *talmidim* from asking questions about points that they did not understand even if their questions were not relevant. He would not let the audience hush a questioner; instead, he would answer with utmost seriousness. When he summarized a *shiur*, reviewing the main points, he would turn to the questioner and say, "And now everything is answered and fits, thanks to your question."

In 1949, while he was giving a *shiur* on *bererah*, a *talmid* asked a difficult question. Rav Chaim stopped the *shiur* and stood in silence for some minutes wiping his forehead. After some thought, he said, "You have asked a very good question. I have to look into this." He did not continue with the principle he was trying to establish but with a completely different one. The *shiur* worked out without the "missing" principle. That night at home, he was immersed in thinking about the question. Eventually he sent a family member with a message to the *talmid*. "You are right. It is a question without an answer. I retract my words."

Once, after a *shiur*, a *talmid* with a Gemara in his hand approached Rav Chaim. From the *talmid's* stance, he understood that the *talmid* was about to ask a question about the Gemara he was holding. Rav Chaim, taking a quick glance at the Gemara's binding, said, "Oh, *Bava Kama?* That's no question," and immediately answered the question that had not yet been asked, at length.

A *talmid* once asked him a question on an explicit *Tosafos* in *Gittin* that apparently contradicted his *shiur*. He eventually received an original and sharp reply. Rav Chaim told him to look in a certain chapter in *Shaagas Aryeh*. The *bochur* looked into the *Shaagas Aryeh*, but he could not find any connection between the subject matter discussed there and the *shiur*. Rav Chaim told him to keep looking in the *Shaagas Aryeh*. This exchange repeated itself until the *bochur* decided to learn the chapter in *Shaagas Aryeh* in depth. After studying it, he concluded that there was still no connection between the *Shaagas Aryeh* and the *shiur*, but that the *Shaagas Aryeh* contradicted that very *Tosafos* in *Gittin*. Still frustrated, he returned to Rav Chaim, arguing that there was no connection between the *Shaagas Aryeh* and the *shiur*. He also mentioned that the *Shaagas Aryeh* contradicted the *Tosafos* in *Gittin*. "If the *Shaagas Aryeh* could write an entire chapter, in the face of the fact that *Tosafos* in *Gittin* contradicts him, I can also say my *shiur*, even if *Tosafos* in *Gittin* apparently contradicts it," Rav Chaim answered him, with some amusement.

For many years, Rav Chaim was particular to preserve the principles that structured the format and content of his *shiurim*. In later years, he did make slight changes in the style of the *shiurim*. "When one gets older, one sees that the simpler is the better," he used to say. In his later *shiurim*, he moderated the *pilpul* and *charifus* elements and concentrated on the understanding and explanation of the subject matter.

From the time of his arrival in Yerushalayim, other *yeshivos* emptied out each time he gave a *shiur*; in fact, all *b'nei Torah* in Yerushalayim streamed to the Mir to enjoy Rav Chaim's genius. Strong students and weak students, those with good memories and those with poor memories—all understood and remembered Rav Chaim's *shiurim*. His unique format and delivery sharpened the minds of his listeners, deepened their self-confidence, and left them with the feeling of having gained something. His *talmidim* would make their own contributions to his *shiurim*, and thus bring his hope that they would "hear and add" to fruition, as the Midrash says and the Gra explains (see chap. 4).

Rav Chaim was well aware that his audience was comprised of people who had different standards and were at different levels. He always minimized the importance of brain-power as a precondition to success in learning, but he did view memory as instrumental. To those with weak memories, he stressed the supreme importance of memory to learning. To those with strong memories, he stressed that one should not rely on memory, but constantly look in the *sefer*. He made great efforts not to give the impression he was quoting by heart, sometimes pretending to read from a piece of a paper on his lap. He would lean over his Gemara and "read" a long piece from it slowly, while only a few knew that the Gemara was not even opened to the correct page! When he gave a passage from memory—usually when the quote was not direct but contained his understanding of it—he would stand upright, bang his finger on the *shtender*, and announce firmly, "Please look inside. Don't rely on me. I'm not asking you to believe me."

There is no time in life in which one enjoys greater happiness than in those days [when the embryo is in its mother's womb]. For it is said [*Iyov* 29:2], O, that I were as in the months of old, as in the days when God watched over me.

(*Niddah* 30b)

It takes me three minutes to eat a meal. An embryo in its mother's womb doesn't even need this—he studies Torah without interruption. That's what Iyov meant when he said, "O, that I were as in the months of old."

(Rav Chaim Shmulevitz)

EIGHT

CONTINUITY

EXERTION AND REVIEW were at the top of Rav Chaim's scale of values. When he spoke of diligence, he meant uninterrupted learning without one minute of time wasted. He discussed the principle of continuity in connection with the Gemara (*Nedarim* 50a) which relates how Rabbi Akiva returned home after twelve years of study. He was already standing in the doorway when he heard Rochel, his wife, say, "If he would listen to me, he would go and learn for another twelve years." Rabbi Akiva immediately turned around and went back to the yeshiva for another twelve years without spending even a minute at home.

Where was his gratitude? Why didn't he enter his home for just a moment to cheer up his poor wife, who had sacrificed the best years of her life for his benefit? Didn't Rabbi Akiva say about her, "Mine and yours are in fact hers"? She had transformed him from a shepherd into Rabbi Akiva!

I think that the decision not to enter his home was
the most difficult halachic ruling that Rabbi Akiva had
to make in his lifetime. He had to be convinced that
during twelve years of learning he had not used one
single minute for himself. If he had, he would have had
to remain at home an equal length of time, for that time
would have belonged to her. If he had used any time
for his own personal benefit and then not spent an
equivalent amount of time with his wife, his halachic
ruling would have been false *(a falsher psak)*.

But what would have been so terrible if Rabbi Akiva
had entered his house? The *Mesilas Yesharim* warns of
the great danger that lies in delaying a mitzvah. Rabbi
Akiva had already heard his wife say that she would
have him go and learn for another twelve years;
entering his house would have been a delay in the
fulfillment of a mitzvah. See how the holy *Chazal*
behaved. The Gemara relates that towards the end of
Rabbi Shimon bar Yochai's wedding, Rav Chananya
ben Chachinai left to learn in the yeshiva. Rabbi
Shimon bar Yochai pleaded with him to wait so that he
could come too, but Rav Chananya refused. What do
you think they would have done together? Without
doubt, they would have learned together *b'chavrusa*.

But one doesn't delay a mitzvah—even for a *chavrusa* like Rabbi Shimon bar Yochai. There is a frightening
moral to this story, and it is an obvious one. Today he
wants to go to learn Torah, but tomorrow? Who knows
what will be? After all, the *Mesilas Yesharim* says the
greatest danger is in delay. Rabbi Akiva also knew this
lesson—it is forbidden to enter his home, the danger is
too great.

Rav Chaim used this gemara to establish one of his most famous principles:

Rabbi Akiva studied twelve years before going home and another twelve years after he returned to the yeshiva. How many years did he learn altogether? Twenty-four. Do you know why the total is twenty-four? Because he did not enter his house. If he had entered his house and interrupted his learning for even one minute, he would have studied twelve years and a further twelve years, but not twenty-four! When there is an interruption in Torah study, twelve plus twelve does not make twenty-four.

In this context, Rav Chaim explained how a *kabbalah* (acceptance of a commitment) transforms a period of time into one continuous unit. He used this principle to emphasize the importance of making *kabbolos* in spiritual matters.

A *nazir* reaches a spiritual level of prophecy after observing thirty days of *nezirus* [*Baal HaTurim, Bamidbar* 6:6]. Someone who refrains from drinking wine, however, is a "sinner." Why? The *kabbalah* of *nezirus* transforms the thirty day period into one unit, and the continuity contained within it gives rise to this tremendous spiritual power.

Someone who abstains from eating for one day is a "sinner," but someone who fasts for one day is "holy" [*Taanis* 11a]. If a person doesn't eat for a day, it has no significance—he simply doesn't eat for one hour, then for another hour, then for another hour, and so on. But a person who accepts a *taanis* doesn't eat for an *entire* day; the *kabbalah* unifies the hours, transforming them into one continuous unit.

Rav Chaim emphasized the rewards of uninterrupted study as much as he emphasized the negative effects of interrupted study.

In a moment of wasted time, one sees the darkness. A moment wasted sends a person sliding down the hill of failure. *Chazal* tell us that the measure of a good deed exceeds the measure of a bad deed. We are, therefore, forced to say that a single moment of Torah study takes a person to unbelievable heights.

The significance of the concept of continuity could be learned just from being in Rav Chaim's presence. As soon as a *chaburah* finished, even before the *talmidim* had a chance to leave the room, he was totally immersed in something else. There was not a second in the day that his mind was not pondering the "problems of Abaye and Rava." While traveling to a wedding, or even to the beach at holiday time, he would prepare his *shiur* or *chaburah*, or turn over some difficult subject in his mind. The veins in his forehead would swell, his face would shine with perspiration, and a smile of infinite pleasure and joy would play at the corners of his mouth.

He usually ate his meals while learning with a *chavrusa,* and he never spent more than four or five minutes eating. Even while eating, he would listen to his *chavrusa's* comments between bites or think with great concentration. At Shabbos meals he would sit deep in thought. During the period when he ate his meals at his father-in-law's home, a *chavrusa,* who would learn with him between courses, used to wait for him in another room. Once, at the beginning of a meal, Rav

Chaim's grandson asked him a question which he had heard from a famous *Yerushalmi maggid*. Rav Chaim sat deep in thought. At the end of the meal, he turned to his grandson and asked, "What answer did he give?" It was obvious he had been thinking about the question the whole time.

Every Shabbos, after davening, it would take a few minutes for the family to gather for the meal. Rav Chaim learned with a *chavrusa* until everyone was seated around the table.

In Kaidan, someone once invited himself to Rav Chaim's house for Shabbos lunch. After davening, the guest remained behind in shul for a few minutes to talk to someone. A quarter of an hour later Rav Chaim returned to the shul. The guest thought that he had come to fetch him. "I am sorry I was delayed," apologized the guest. "I am coming immediately." "The meal is awaiting you," answered Rav Chaim. "If you want to eat with me, you will have to come to the third meal, for I have already finished lunch."

Despite the brevity of his meals, eating played an important spiritual role in his life. He was always particular to eat at the same table at which he studied, in the nicest room in the apartment.

A table is compared to an altar—only fools take the altar out of the living room and into the kitchen.

*   *   *

Rav Chaim spent many sleepless nights pondering questions to which he had not yet found answers. When he sat down in the morning to learn with his *chavrusa* he would say, "I did not sleep last night—I found a new approach to the *sugya*."

On many occasions, when he was not able to come to a satisfactory conclusion about a particular *sugya* and felt that the subject matter was still somewhat confused, he would say, "I will go to sleep. While I sleep, we'll see what will come out." *(Shloffendik vellen mir zehen vos vert arois kumen fun dem.)* Then later he would testify that, indeed, it had all sorted itself out while he slept. One family member remembers Rav Chaim taking a nap before a *shiur* and awaking with an idea that had come to him while he slept. He eagerly repeated the idea to himself and conveyed it to his *talmidim*.

There was not a day of the year on which he did not learn: Purim, *erev* Yom Kippur, Yom Kippur, *erev* Pesach, *motzo'ei* Simchas Torah…During the days immediately preceding Pesach, when Pesach cleaning was at its height and furniture was being moved to and fro, he learned outside the house. During Chol HaMoed Pesach, he hid away with a *chavrusa* in another apartment so Yom Tov visitors would not disturb him.

Rav Chaim angrily decried the prevalent laxity in learning on Fridays and *Shabbosim*:

> Torah is to be learned every day, including Friday and Shabbos. When the yeshiva is empty, a tremendous amount of Torah that can easily be acquired lays around.

In *shmuessen*, especially those he gave at the beginning of the *zman*, he emphasized the importance of learning in the yeshiva *beis hamedrash*. "Even learning in the *ezras nashim* is prohibited," he used to note. He himself was very particular to learn in the yeshiva on Shabbos. (He also remarked to his married *chavrusos* that home is not a refuge from learning and that one could also learn and *shteig* there.) In one of the *shmuessen* he gave at the beginning of a *zman*, he described entering the empty *beis hamedrash* during *bein hazmanim* and hearing the "Gemara crying." The audience was moved to tears.

Rav Chaim spent most of the day learning with a *chavrusa*, and, except for the few hours he slept or wrote, he was always in the company of *talmidim*. He viewed learning with a *chavrusa* as the embodiment of an important spiritual principle, one which he often emphasized in his actions and in his *shmuessen*:

This is the way of creation: He who takes for himself and does not encourage his friend to participate...what he himself has is taken away from him.

It is written in *Shemos* [22:24-26]: "When you lend money to [one of] my people...do not press him for repayment....If you take your neighbor's garment as security for a loan, you must return it to him before sunset. This alone is his covering, the garment for his skin. With what shall he sleep? Therefore, if he cries out to Me, I will listen, for I am compassionate."

Why is the borrower "crying out"? What injustice was done to him? He borrowed money and cannot return it. God also wants a Jew to return the money that he borrowed. Indeed, no injustice was done to him—he is not crying out about injustice. He is crying out because he is upset. But why should the lender suffer because the borrower is upset? Surely this is a matter between the borrower and God. The *Sforno* explains, "When 'he cries out to Me' about his poverty, I will give him a little of what I was going to give you, in excess of your needs, which you were to use to support others." An amazing insight! A person is only given more than his basic needs in order to support others! And when "he cries out to Me, I will listen"— since you have more than you need, and you are still pressuring someone else. Therefore, I will take the excess away from you and give it to the other person.

This idea is stated explicitly in *Mishlei*: "The rich
and the poor meet together. *Hashem* is the maker of
them all." The Gemara [*Temurah* 16b] explains: "When
the poor man goes to the donor and says 'assist me,' and
he assists him, all is well. But if he does not assist him,
'the rich and poor meet together.' He who made this one
rich can make him poor, and He who made this one
poor can make him rich."

Rashi comments on the words, "*Hashem* is the
maker of them all": "'Maker of them all'—anew."
Whatever you have, it is only for now. What will be in
a moment from now? In the next moment *Hashem*
makes everything anew.

The same is true in spiritual matters. See what
Chazal say a few lines earlier: "The poor man and the
man of medium wealth have met together. *Hashem*
lightens both their eyes" [*Mishlei* 29:13]. Who is the
poor man? *Chazal* tells us that he is a man poor in
Torah, a *talmid*. Who is the man of medium wealth?
Rashi explains in his commentary on the Gemara that
the man of medium wealth is one who knows two or
three *sedarim* of *Shass*, or, in the words of *Chazal*, "the
rebbe." When a *talmid* asks his rebbe to teach him
Torah and the rebbe agrees, *Hashem* lightens both their
eyes. Both still need to learn, and *Hashem* teaches both
of them. But if the rebbe learns alone and does not teach
others, see what happens: "The rich and the poor meet
together." He who made this one wise can make him a
fool, and He who made this one a fool can make him
wise.

See what *Chazal* teach us. Your teachers have given
you knowledge, they have given you the ability to teach
someone else—why do you take it all for yourself?
"*Hashem* is the maker of them all."

The Gemara [*Taanis* 7a] says, " 'A sword is upon the solitary, and they shall become fools' [*Yirmiyahu* 50:36]. Destruction shall come upon scholars who study alone...." Such people deserve to die! It is not a punishment, however; they simply forfeit their right to live. The Gemara continues, "Destruction comes upon those scholars who study alone, and even worse, they become stultified." Foolishness is worse than death.

The Rambam knew what foolishness was. In his introduction to *Seder Zeraim,* he cites the Gemara: "Anyone who mocks the words of the *chachomim* is punished [in the next world] with boiling excrement." In *that* world, a person is shown clearly what type of filth he is boiling in. Do we think that this refers only to the suffering of *gehinnom*? No, *Rabosai.* The Rambam adds a few words: "There is no greater boiling excrement than foolishness." Foolishness is the boiling excrement of this world! Such a boiling excrement does not even exist there!

"And even worse, they become stultified." This is the worst *gehinnom.* You are afraid of the *gehinnom* there? See what a *gehinnom* one can have here, and for what reason! Because a person studies Torah alone, without a *chavrusa*! These are simple facts for a person to understand.

Nasan HaNavi came to Dovid HaMelech and told him the parable of the lamb: The rich man, who has everything, took the poor man's only lamb. Did he take it for himself? No! He took it to fulfill the mitzvah of *hachnosas orchim* [*Shmuel* 2 12:4]. What does Dovid HaMelech rule? "This man shall die." I will tell you the truth. I reviewed the entire Torah and could not find the death penalty for theft anywhere. Why does this

man deserve to die? The answer is as we have explained. When a person takes something for himself,
even to do a mitzvah, he is not given the death penalty;
it is not a punishment. He simply forfeits the right to
live.

I can prove this principle from *Chazal*.

"What was the sin of Nadav and Avihu? Bar Kapara
says, '"Aharon's sons, Nadav and Avihu, each took
their fire pan." They did not take advice from each
other'" [*VaYikra Rabbah* 20:66].

See how *Chazal* understand a *posuk* in *Tanach*.
When Eliyahu parted from Elisha [*Melochim* 2 2:11], it
says:

"And as they were walking and talking, behold a
chariot of fire and horses of fire appeared and separated
them from each other, and Eliyahu went up in a
whirlwind into heaven." What do *Chazal* say about this
posuk? "If two *talmidei chachomim* are going on a
journey and there are no words of Torah between them,
they deserve to be burned with fire. We learn this from
Eliyahu and Elisha" [*Sotah* 41b]. What does the Gemara
say? "And there are no words of Torah *between them*."
They may both be deeply immersed in a *sugya*, but if
there are no words of Torah between them, if each one
is thinking only for himself, they deserve to be burned.
The *posuk* says, "And...they were walking and talking."
Chazal deduce that because they were talking, they
were not burned, but if they had not been talking, they
would have been burned. They could both have been
thinking about matters as profound as *maaseh mer-
kavah*, but if they had not communicated with each
other, if they had not learned *together*, they would have
deserved to be burned. Eliyahu went up to heaven in a

whirlwind. Why were a chariot and horses of fire necessary? Rashi says, "Because they would have deserved to be burned had they not been talking together."

This is also the meaning of Bar Kapara's statement. Nadav and Avihu were each *mechadesh* a *chiddush*, an "unauthorized fire that God had not commanded." They believed that they could improve themselves spiritually by doing this, but they did not communicate their *chiddush* to each other. Therefore, a fire came down and consumed them. They did not deserve to live. Torah was not given for a person to take for himself.

A mute person, who hears but cannot speak, is not obligated in the mitzvah of *hakhel*. Why? Because the purpose of *hakhel* is "that they may hear and they may learn" [*Devarim* 31:12]. Rashi explains that a mute person, who cannot teach someone else, is exempt because he cannot learn. This in spite of the fact that the spiritual elevation that resulted from the mitzvah of *hakhel* was enormous. The women and even the children were all there....*Chazal* relate how two mute people were cured and were found to know all of *Halacha*, *Sifra*, *Sifri*, and *Shass*. And it is just such mute people who are excluded from the mitzvah because "they cannot learn." This is mind shattering! If you are attending *hakhel* to learn for yourself, stay at home!

See what the Torah says about Avraham in connection with Sodom. "God said, 'Shall I conceal from Avraham what I am going to do? Avraham is to become a great and mighty nation....I have given him special attention so he will command his children and his household after him....'" [*Bereshis* 18:17-19]. *Hashem* wanted to teach Avraham an important lesson about *middas hadin*. But is it Avraham who deserves to be taught in his own right? No, *Rabosai*. Avraham is being taught only because he will become a great nation and teach it to his children. The Torah was not given to him to keep for himself.

When Rav Chaim spoke about the advantages of learning with a *chavrusa*, he would connect this idea with the concept of joint responsibility and the importance of people being close to one another.

When Moshe Rabbenu saw the burning bush, he said, "I must go over there and investigate this wonderful phenomenon." When God saw that Moshe was going to investigate, He called to him from the middle of the bush. "Going to investigate" was the reason why Moshe was made the special leader of *Klal Yisroel* and merited to receive the Torah. But *Chazal* reveal that "going to investigate" does not refer to the bush, but to the people's suffering—"he went to see their suffering and share their yoke" [*Shemos Rabbah* 2:66]. Sharing with others is one of the forty-eight ways in which Torah is acquired.

Concerning learning with a *chavrusa*, Rav Chaim cited the gemara in *Sukkah* 45b:

"Rav Yirmiyah said in the name of Rabbi Shimon bar Yochai, 'I can exempt the whole world from judgment from the day I was born until now.' " I don't know how old Rabbi Shimon bar Yochai was. Let us assume that he was fifty or sixty years old. " 'And were Eliezer, my son, with me, we could exempt it from the day of the creation of the world to the present time.' " I ask,

Rabosai, where is the proportion? Rabbi Shimon him-self could exempt the whole world from judgment for only a few decades, but with his son, he could exempt the world from judgment from the day it was created—thousands of years. I haven't seen anywhere that his son was greater than he was.

See the power of *chavrusa.* Do we begin to under-stand the significance of two people learning together? The Gemara continues, " '...and were Yosam ben Uz-ziah with us, we could exempt it from its creation to its final end.' " See the power of a group of people learning together.

At the beginning of every *zman,* Rav Chaim spoke about the importance of learning with a *chavrusa.* "How can one sit and learn quietly and peacefully knowing that his friend does not have a *chavrusa?*" he would shout. When a *talmid* asked him to arrange a *chavrusa* for him, Rav Chaim would answer, "If, by tomorrow, I am not able to find a *chavrusa* for you, I will learn with you myself." This, indeed, sometimes hap-pened.

*   *   *

Rav Eliezer also said: "Be always humble, so that you may endure." Rav Zeira said: "We have learned likewise. 'The windows of a dark house may not be opened to examine it for leprosy.' " [If leprosy breaks out in the walls of a house, and the priest coming to examine it finds the house too dark for a proper survey, the windows may not be opened to allow light to enter. The room must be examined by its usual light. Thus, its darkness protects it; in the absence of a proper examination, the house cannot be pronounced unclean. Similarly, the darkness in which a man wraps himself, i.e., humility, protects his life.]

(Sanhedrin 92a)

See how Rav Zeira understood this halacha. When it is dark, one doesn't look and one doesn't search.

(Rav Chaim Shmulevitz)

The friendliness and deep brotherly feelings that Rav Chaim showed to every individual were marked by their simplicity and humility. He never allowed anyone to wait on him. He would wave away those who tried to accompany him when he walked in the street. Even toward the end of his life, when every step was painful, he refused to allow anyone to bring him tea from the kitchen. For as long as possible, he tried not to be a burden to his fellow man. He would say thank you for every favor. Even when he asked one of his children to do something for him, he introduced the request with the words, "Please, trouble yourself" (*bemizach*). While he still had the strength, he would take books out of his bookcase himself. Later, when he was weaker, if there was a child in the room, he would ask him to bring a book so as not to trouble his *chavrusa*.

For a long time, the telephone in the yeshiva was the only one in the neighborhood. When a neighbor received a call, Rav Chaim would go and summon him, even if that neighbor lived a distance from the yeshiva. When a *bochur* was called to the telephone, and there was no child available to go and find him, Rav Chaim would interrupt his learning and go to call the *bochur* himself.

When he learned with a *chavrusa*, all barriers dropped. He would inquire after his health and that of his family, and if any problems arose, he would do his utmost to help and advise the *chavrusa*.

When he was asked to be *mesader kiddushin*, he would go to great lengths to find out if there was someone else whom it would be more suitable to honor. When he came to a wedding and saw another *rosh yeshiva* standing near the *chupah*, he refused to be *mesader kiddushin*. He was once invited to be *mesader kiddushin* in a faraway settlement, hours from Yerushalayim. When he arrived, he heard one of the young people ask innocently, "Why isn't the local rabbi *mesader kiddushin*?" Fearful that the local rabbi would refuse to be *mesader kiddushin* if he knew he was there, Rav Chaim immediately turned around and traveled back to Yerushalayim.

He would always refuse to be *sandek* if there was a grandfather or some other worthy relative to whom it was fitting to give the honor.

If someone ordered a private taxi for him, he would always object: "What do I care if there are another fifty people traveling with me?" He would always allow his *talmidim* to enter a bus ahead of him and would often pay for their tickets.

A *bochur* once came to apply for admission to the yeshiva. He was met by Rav Chaim, who took him to his father-in-law, the *rosh yeshiva*, Rav Laizer Yudel Finkel. He carried the *bochur's* suitcases up the stairs, and when the *bochur* left the *rosh yeshiva's* room and announced joyfully that he had been accepted, Rav Chaim again lifted up the suitcases and brought him to his room. The *talmid* asked him, "What is your function and position here in the yeshiva?" Rav Chaim answered, "I'm the *shammas*."

He never made a fuss about himself. He did not view his great achievements as anything personal. He often stated publicly that the greatness of a person derives from the power of the community. If a community believes in a person, he grows and becomes great because of that belief. He always underestimated the influence of his *shmuessen* on his audience. On being told that a particular *shmuess* was outstanding, he answered, "You only want to give me pleasure." It was hard work to convince him that his *shmuessen* had any influence at all. When a collection of his *shmuessen* sold out within a few days of publication, he was amazed. Before publication, he had argued vehemently that nobody would want to buy the book. When he was told that the book was selling rapidly, he sighed and said, "Obviously this is due to *zechus avos*."

He was very energetic, never allowing time to pass between an idea and its practical application. After it became difficult for him to walk, he would bemoan the fact that he was unable to translate many of his ideas into action. He would often say, "If only I could, I would have gotten up and done something about this." Once, the wife of a friend from Shanghai came to the yeshiva and asked Rav Chaim to daven for her small son who had diphtheria. As soon as he heard the story, Rav Chaim ran to his friend's house, took the sick child in his arms, and carried him to the hospital. There he made sure that the child received treatment befitting a patient who had a *rosh yeshiva* looking after his welfare.

He would feed his children and grandchildren and often take them to play with their friends. Once he took his daughter to play with a friend and discovered that the friend lived in a house with a courtyard that opened onto the street. Rav Chaim was afraid that the girls would run into the street. He stood at the door of the courtyard in such a manner that she couldn't see him while she was playing and feel uncomfortable, and he watched to make sure they didn't run into the street. He stood there immersed in a difficult *sugya* until it was time to take his daughter home.

Rav Chaim managed to combine greatness and simplicity, and his *talmidim* and relatives became familiar with both qualities. It is not unusual for someone who feels at home with a great person to become so familiar with his greatness that he begins to overlook it. Rav Chaim himself often cited the gemara in *Sanhedrin* 52b: "How is the scholar regarded by the ignorant man? At first like a golden ladle. If he converses with him, like a silver ladle. If he derives benefit from him, like an earthenware ladle, which cannot be mended once it is broken." He would elaborate and describe every stage in the deterioration of the perception of greatness that the ignorant man has of the *talmid chochom,* until closeness and familiarity transform the *talmid chochom* into a broken earthenware ladle in the eyes of the *am ha'aretz.*

But Rav Chaim's greatness always managed to overcome the familiarity that weakens respect. Not one *talmid* or family member ever lost respect for his greatness, notwithstanding the closeness they felt toward him and he felt toward them.

Rav Chaim was lying in the hospital. A patient suffering from a painful illness was brought into his room. With the little strength left in him, with a shaking hand, Rav Chaim managed to commit to paper the pain he felt at witnessing the other man's suffering. "When one is suffering, it is easier to identify with the suffering of another."

NINE

YISSURIM

R AV CHAIM suffered his entire life. He was hard of hearing from early youth. Over the years, he lost the hearing in one ear entirely and most of the hearing in his other ear. He needed an aid to hear anything at all, and even then he constantly heard a buzzing sound, which worsened as the years went by. He had a weak heart, high blood pressure, and suffered from bad migraine headaches. In addition, he had a weak back, which often caused him excruciating pain.

Later in life he suffered a stroke, which affected his throat and mouth, and he never fully recovered from it. Despite this weakness, he continued to say his *shiur*. The following anecdote illustrates his extreme self-sacrifice and devotion to saying his *shiur*. Once Rav Chaim lost consciousness. A doctor rushed to his bedside and managed to revive him. When he regained consciousness, he realized that it was time to say his *shiur*, but his doctor and family refused to allow him to go to the yeshiva. He complained to his *chavrusa*, "In the last twenty-four years, I've missed saying my *shiur* four times, but this time it was my fault."

Even those who did not know of his physical weakness and pain were impressed with the strength which characterized his study of Torah, but those who did know and who were often in his presence were totally amazed and filled with wonder at his self-control. At times he would simply collapse on his bed from exhaustion. Then, when he felt better, he would spring up and sit by the table to learn. When asked how he felt, he would say that he still felt ill, but the fact that he was feeling a little better was enough to get him back to learning.

Even when he was in severe pain, he never delayed or canceled his learning commitments. Many times, his family attempted to dissuade him from saying a *shiur*, *chaburah*, *mussar shmuess*, or a *vaad*, but Rav Chaim was never willing to listen. He used to say, "The only time I can forget my suffering is when I am saying a *shiur*, so what is the point of canceling?"

In his later years, he found it difficult to walk. He had to exert himself to climb the stairs to the yeshiva and go up to the *bimah*. Once he was on the *bimah*, however, his weakness and pain were not noticeable. Then it seemed as if he was completely divorced from his physical being. He refused to allow the waves of suffering to overcome him. All his family's pleadings that it would be impossible for him to say a *shiur* were to no avail. "There is no 'impossible,'" he would respond. When he returned from a *shiur*, he would exclaim with joy, "You see, it was alright. It was possible to say the *shiur*."

Once he collapsed and lost consciousness, and he was not able to talk until half an hour after he was revived. "I had nothing else to do," he said, "so I prepared a *shiur*."

During the Shanghai years, he contracted typhoid and could not learn. One of his *talmidim* tried to comfort him by recalling that a person under duress is free from his obligations *(ones rachmanah patrei)*. Rav Chaim was shocked. "How can one talk that way about Torah study!" he exclaimed.

On many occasions, when his strength was completely consumed, he would say to his *talmidim*, "Look further into this *sugya*, I'm going to hear what my pillow has to say." Then he would get up from the table and go to his room to lie down. Never more than seven or eight minutes later, he would return with renewed strength, his youthful spirit continuing to find new *chiddushei Torah*.

His physical strength never determined the amount of time he spent learning. On the contrary, learning seemed to increase his physical strength. Given the large number of *chaburos* and *vaadim* he gave, the difficulty he had speaking, due to the damage the stroke had done to his throat, constituted a terrible physical burden. But his great spiritual strength stood by him.

On the day of his youngest son's wedding, when everyone was ready to leave for the wedding hall, Rav Chaim called for one of the *talmidim* from the yeshiva, an older student who was still unmarried. He sat with the *talmid* for a long time, discussing various topics related to marriage. "Today," Rav Chaim said to the *talmid*, "I'm marrying off my youngest son. My happiness is great, and I thought to myself, 'Whom should I think about on this day, when I take my youngest son to the *chuppah?*' I'm thinking about you."

TEN

I'M THINKING ABOUT YOU

R AV CHAIM'S CHILDHOOD was full of pain and wandering, his leadership years, permeated with danger. But no *nisayon* ever succeeded in cooling the ardor of his heart. As a child, he was known to be obstinate; when he grew up, he became a man of principle.

The years of shouldering responsibility, the years of being the yeshiva's pillar of strength in dangerous situations, developed the aggressive side of his personality. It is only natural that although difficult situations and constant conflict weaken a person, they also immunize him and this immunization helps him withstand difficulties—man's nature is such that he has the ability to adapt to all situations. The finer senses that are buried deep in his personality, however, can become blurred and dissipated; excitement and shock can cause a lessening of sensitivity and intensity of emotion. Rav Chaim himself once gave a detailed presentation on this very theme. Among other sources, he cited the gemara (*Yoma* 23a) which relates how numerous murders in the days of Menasheh dulled the people's deep, natural abhorrence of murder for many years.

Rav Chaim overcame this natural human tendency to develop a dulling of sensitivity. His personality embodied two extremes. On the one hand, he was a man of intellect, logic, understanding, and intellectual flexibility, who could understand any subject from many perspectives. On the other hand, he was a man of extreme sensitivity, whose emotional responses, undiminished by his trials, at times reached the level of real pain and suffering. There toiled within him acute sensitivity and resoluteness, both of which were infectious. Only a pure Torah personality like Rav Chaim's was able to encompass cold intellect—albeit awake and lively—and vibrant, human emotion. His personality contained these two contradictory traits, yet managed to synthesize them, and this synthesis led to his uniqueness.

When it came to human suffering, Rav Chaim was able to separate all the side issues that could weaken one's sympathy for another person's misery and cut through them to *the* central issue—the other person's suffering. He was able to apply the same power he had in the intricacies of Torah to human sensitivity—to turn what seemed like a detail into a general principle, to view emotional and halachic issues in exactly the same way.

Because of his deafness, Rav Chaim would stand beside the *baal koreh* when the Torah was read. The *baal koreh* would hear Rav Chaim weep when he read the *parsha* about the sale of Yosef or the *haftorah* about Chanah and Peninah. When *Megilas Rus* was read, Rav Chaim would cry bitterly. On Yom Kippur, when the *piyut* describing the death of the ten martyrs was recited, and on Tishah B'Av, when it was recited again as as a *kinah,* his tears would pour forth in a flood. The description of the sufferings of Rabbi Akiva and the daughter of Kalba Savua also caused him great emotional distress. On one occasion, during a *shmuess* in which he was explaining different sayings of *Chazal* on the subject at length, his entire body was suddenly struck with a bitter attack of crying. The tears choked his throat, and he was unable to continue the *shmuess* for a long time.

His youngest son was born during the Israeli War of Independence. The *bris milah* took place in the hospital, as exploding shells shook the walls. The shells were still falling when Rav Chaim made his way home, running from doorway to doorway. In one house, he noticed a small child whose hands and legs were bandaged. He stopped and began to cry. One of his relatives shouted after him to hurry and take cover, but Rav Chaim could not move. He stood there looking at the suffering child, ignoring the fact that he himself was in mortal danger.

The importance of feeling another's pain was one of Rav Chaim's major themes:

Fools think that sharing a person's burden simply means helping him. They think that once an injured person has been treated, and he again can do things on his own, it is no longer possible to "help" him, even though his injury may still cause him pain. If "help" means physical help, how can one help someone after he has been treated? Sharing another person's burden means sharing his pain and suffering. When he is carrying a heavy load, everybody understands the necessity of lending a hand. When he is carrying a heavy load of pain and anguish, one has to lend a heart. See what *Chazal* say: "If he [the sufferer] is a *talmid chochom*, one has to feel sick about him." Do *Chazal* speak of help? Do *Chazal* say, "Bring him a cup of tea"? *Chazal* say, "One has to feel sick about him." Take his pain into your heart, feel his suffering, and if he is a *talmid chochom*, become sick from feeling the pain of his suffering.

But does this help? Of course it helps. Have you ever seen a group of people in pain? When one person is in mourning, he carries the entire burden on his shoulders. When two people are in mourning, it's easier for them. They divide the pain between them. This is man's nature. Referring to Iyov, God says to the *satan*, "But protect his soul." God allowed the *satan* to take everything away from Iyov, but He didn't allow the *satan* to take his friends away from him. If Iyov had suffered alone, he wouldn't have been able to stand it. When he was with others, the pain and suffering was divided among all of them. The Gemara [*Bava Basra* 16b] says, "Either a friend like the friends of Iyov or death." Man cannot suffer alone and survive.

When Rav Chaim heard that someone had taken ill, he would burst out crying. Sometimes he would walk up and down in his room, ill at ease, unable to calm himself. When he himself was weak and sick, his family had to hide newspaper obituaries from him, for they affected his health. When he was dying, and in extreme pain, he constantly asked about the health of others. Whenever he listened to the personal problems of one of his *talmidim*, he inquired about the details at length, then waited until the *talmid* left the room before he cried for a long period of time. He was usually careful not to cry in front of people who came to tell him of their suffering, so as not to add to their pain.

A certain blind man attended Rav Chaim's funeral. When people asked him why he had come, the blind man replied, "When I went to speak to Rav Chaim, he inquired after my health. I told him that the doctors had said there was no hope for my eyesight, and he cried for twenty minutes."

On his deathbed, Rav Chaim heard that a famous *talmid chochom* was a patient in another part of the hospital. Despite his own illness, he insisted that he be taken to visit the sick *talmid chochom.* Those who were with him tried to dissuade him—every movement he made caused him suffering and anguish—but he would not listen. He was taken in a wheel-chair to the room of the sick *talmid chochom.* There, he quietly wept and prayed at the head of the bed.

On the last Hoshanah Rabbah of his life, a visitor came to see him in the hospital. When the visitor left, Rav Chaim asked for his clothes. At that point, his health was deteriorating rapidly and the very idea that he wanted to go somewhere frightened those around him. They could not even get him to explain his insistence on being given his clothes. Rav Chaim was obstinate. With great difficulty, he dressed and insisted that a taxi be called to take him to the *kosel.* At the *kosel,* he took from his pocket a piece of paper on which he had written the name of the sick person for whom he had been asked to pray. With his last strength, he finished praying and returned to the hospital.

Rav Chaim did not believe in suppressing emotions. One *erev* Shabbos, the daughter of one of his *talmidim* was slightly injured in a terrorist attack. On Sunday morning, the *talmid* came to learn *chavrusa* with Rav Chaim as if nothing had happened. He did not bother to tell him about his daughter's injury. When Rav Chaim heard the story, he burst into tears. "A cold-hearted father" *(a kalter tatte),* he said.

At the time of the Entebbe hijacking in 1976, he was ill and in great pain. Nevertheless, he turned over worlds with his prayers and cries that the community should strengthen itself. Before, when one of the great *roshei yeshiva* was captured by Palestinian terrorists and held captive for a month, Rav Chaim traveled about the country on a speaking tour. In every *shmuess* he admonished his audience not to rest or be silent, but to open the heavens with their prayers. He described the *rosh yeshiva* as a *godol b'Torah*, a community leader, and, he emphasized most, a *mashpiah*. In his *hesped* for one of the *gedolei Yisroel* who died at that time, Rav Chaim begged the deceased to go before the heavenly throne and act as an advocate for the captured *rosh yeshiva*. Long after his release, the *rosh yeshiva* related, in one of his *shmuessen*, how he had been amazed by Rav Chaim's extreme joy when they met— nearly two years after he was freed!

When his brother-in-law, the Gaon and Tzaddik Rav Chaim Zev Finkel, became ill, Rav Chaim could find no rest. His wailing and crying shook every heart. In a *shmuess* he gave in the yeshiva at that time, he said, "Do you think that while my brother-in-law is lying on his deathbed, it's easy for me to speak?...My heart is bleeding." When he entered the yeshiva and opened the *aron hakodesh*, his heartrending prayers seemed to pierce the heavens. This continued for nine months. As his brother-in-law's condition worsened, the community resigned itself to the situation and prepared for the worst. Rav Chaim, however, with a tirelessness that will always be remembered by the yeshiva's students, continued to make everyone's heart tremble with his calls for prayer: "How can one become used to the situation?" he shouted. "How can one become used to it?"

When any of the *gedolei Yisroel* became ill, Rav Chaim was sure to take part in organized communal prayers at the *kosel*. Some months before his *petirah*, he even changed the time of his *shiur* from evening to afternoon in order to participate in a communal prayer.

The prayers he recited at the graves of *tzaddikim* are a subject in themselves. On one of his journeys to the Galil, he visited the graves of Rabbi Shimon bar Yochai, Rabbi Meir

Baal Haness, the Rambam, and the Ridvaz. He commented that the feeling of connection is stronger with a *tzaddik* who lived nearer to our generation, and it is easier to pray at his grave *(si davent zich besser)*. The further in the past the *tzaddik* lived, the stronger the feeling of distance and the harder to pray.

At the graves of some *tzaddikim*, tears poured forth from him like water. When he visited the grave of the Or HaChaim, he would call him rebbe and beg forgiveness for disagreeing with the Or HaChaim's explanations of certain *psukim*. At some graves, he recited special prayers. At the graves of the *avos* at *Me'aras Hamachpelah*, he would make three requests: that the bodies of deceased Jews be brought to their graves without mutilation; that secular Jews merit to see the truth; and that the Jewish people live in its land in peace. He would ask the *avos* to go before the heavenly throne and pray for his welfare. He would speak to them in Yiddish, as if he were speaking to a friend. At *Kever Rochel*, he would cry and say, "Mother Rochel, God says, 'Restrain your voice from weeping, your eyes from tears.' He asks you to refrain from weeping— your son asks you, 'Mother, do not refrain from weeping. Go up before the heavenly throne and ask for mercy for your children, who are in trouble.' "

In a *shmuess* on the night of Yom Kippur, Rav Chaim related how he often went to pray at the graves of the righteous only to sense that his prayers were not being answered. On one visit to the grave of the Or HaChaim, he passed Yad Avshalom. He stopped and stood quietly in front of the monument for a long time, deep in thought. Then, to the surprise of those accompanying him, suddenly he began to pray.

My companions looked at me. "Why are you praying here? Avshalom was a wicked person—a murderer, a sinner. His father, Dovid, had to raise him seven levels to bring him out of *gehinnom.*" I will tell you what I prayed, and it worked. I said, "When a person says to a friend, 'I forgive you,' they are only words. Only when a father says 'I forgive you,' is he really forgiving. Look at how much persecution Dovid HaMelech suffered from that wicked son of his, yet, as a father, he forgave him. *Ribono Shel Olam*, You are our Father and Your forgiveness is forgiveness. Please say, 'I forgive you.'

Rav Chaim's prayers expressed a deep feeling of closeness to God. It was clear that when he stood before God, he felt personally connected to Him. Once, when he was praying at the *kosel*, a bystander heard him say in Yiddish, "*Ribono Shel Olam*, You Yourself, without any intermediaries."

Sometimes, when he could not understand a *sugya* in the Gemara, he would restlessly walk up and down in the *beis hamedrash*, then stop at a front corner of the *aron hakodesh* and say, "*Ribono Shel Olam*, I don't understand the *sugya*. Please help me understand." He would concentrate for a long time and finally walk up to the *aron hakodesh* with a shining face and joyfully say, "Thank You."

Rav Chaim had a tradition from the Chofetz Chaim to speak about Russian Jewry on Yom Kippur night.

A third of the Jewish people are in captivity in Russia. They are prevented from doing *mitzvos*, and they are being pulled away from their roots. Each year that goes by deepens the destruction of Russian Jewry, and every *tefach* added to its depth is, in fact, a completely new destruction.

In those years, when no one dared dream of the possibility that Russian Jews would be allowed to leave Russia, Rav

Chaim stood on the *bimah* of the Mir Yeshiva on Yom Kippur night with a broken heart and called for their release with confidence that it would undoubtedly happen.

On that night, he would speak about all the Jews who are removed from the practice of Judaism. Many years before the *baal teshuvah* movement made its appearance, when the very idea of secular Jews coming back to the practice of Judaism seemed totally impractical, Rav Chaim stood and described a scene of mass return to Jewish practice, something which he maintained, with the mercy of God, was certain to happen. He would ask for compassion for those lost souls. "People should feel their pain and pray to God to open their eyes."

He also spoke about *mitzvos bein odom l'chavero*. In sharp colors, he would describe how a person could pass a Yom Kippur, a day of judgment, without it being a day of atonement. He would emphasize the husband-wife relationship, and he was critical of yeshiva students who left their homes for Yom Kippur and traveled to *yeshivos* to daven. He would cite sources in *Chazal* illustrating that husbands should return home especially on Yom Kippur.

In the last years of his life, on Friday mornings, Rav Chaim gave a special *vaad* to the young married men learning in the yeshiva. Most of this *vaad* concerned the subject of *mitzvos bein adam l'chavero* as they applied to home life.

*   *   *

Who is honored? He who honors others.
(Avos 4:1)

A person who thinks he can be honored without honoring others errs in an explicit law.
(Rav Chaim Shmulevitz)

The great emphasis Rav Chaim placed on the concept of *hakoras ha'tov* (recognizing a debt of gratitude) reveals another facet of his personality. He would take the trouble to travel great distances, sometimes in the cabin of an uncomfortable truck, to participate in the *vort* of a *talmid* from another yeshiva who had honored him by coming to hear his *chaburos*. Every *bochur* who had studied with Rav Chaim received a personal visit from him after marriage. The deeper purpose of this visit was to raise the new wife's esteem for her husband. He would attend every *simchah* to which he was invited in order to reciprocate for the trouble and attention shown by the person who invited him. He was, however, very particular that whoever invited him also invited his wife. When he was offered any refreshment, however light, he would, without fail, thank the hostess before he left her house, even if she was a close family member.

Brief anecdotes like these about Rav Chaim number in the hundreds. Family and *talmidim* recall many occasions when they wondered aloud why he had acted in a certain way. "I have a debt of gratitude toward that person," he would invariably answer.

A *talmid* once escorted him to a *sheva brochos*. When they arrived, Rav Chaim asked the *bochur* to accompany him inside. The *bochur* answered that he first had to go on an errand, which would take about half an hour. Rav Chaim answered, "I will wait for you. I will not wash my hands until you return." Hearing this, the *bochur* decided not to go on his errand. At the *sheva brochos*, Rav Chaim made sure the *bochur* received a good portion and watched him to make sure he was eating well.

The house in which Rav Chaim lived in Shanghai was owned by a very simple Jew. Although Rav Chaim was known as a person who did not indulge in small talk, he would nonetheless spend long hours with the owner in simple conversation which lacked any spiritual content. When his colleagues asked him how he could permit himself to take valuable time away from his learning to make empty conversation with an ignorant man, Rav Chaim answered, "He opened up his house for me. Don't I owe him a debt of gratitude?" That simple man eventually settled in Eretz Yisroel and lived in a city far from Yerushalayim. Rav Chaim traveled to visit him on a number of occasions.

Rav Chaim understood that *mitzvos bein odom l'chavero* were based on far more than simple good-heartedness. Once a *bochur* applied for admission to the yeshiva in the middle of the *zman*. Rav Chaim made detailed inquiries about the *bochur*, particularly since he had left a yeshiva in the middle of the *zman*, and he requested a letter of recommendation from his previous yeshiva. (Letters of recommendation were a hard and fast rule in the Mir Yeshiva. Rav Chaim often stressed that one does not leave a place of learning without asking permission. Any *bochur* who applied to the yeshiva and criticized his previous yeshiva in any way was not accepted.) When, during their conversation, Rav Chaim learned that he was not talking to a *bochur*, but to a recently married young man who was looking for a *kollel*, his reaction changed completely. He gave the young man a very warm and eager welcome, and the whole subject of a letter of recommendation was dropped.

On another occasion, when a *bochur* who made a strange first impression came to apply to the yeshiva, Rav Chaim gently refused him. When the *bochur* left the room, Rav Chaim asked some members of his family if any of them knew the *bochur*. "A strange *bochur*," he mused out loud. Only a few minutes had passed when he sent someone out to find the *bochur* at all costs. To the surprised members of the household, he explained with deep anguish, "I said that he's strange." The *bochur* was accepted to the yeshiva.

Unhappy, depressed, and misfit Jews would often visit him. Although he was disturbed by their visits, he always honored his guests in an exceptional manner. Many of his visitors were older people who had forgotten their learning. He received them with special warmth and treated them with love and infinite patience. One such person came from out of town to visit Rav Chaim from time to time. As soon as he arrived, Rav Chaim would bring him a chair, spread a tablecloth, and lay out a meal for him, all without assistance. He would listen for hours to what the man was saying, even though his conversation was unintelligible.

Rav Chaim returned warm greetings to everyone who greeted him. Once he asked the *talmid* with him, "Who was that?" "From the way the *rosh yeshiva* greeted him, I understood that the *rosh yeshiva* recognized him and knew him," the *talmid* responded. "No," said Rav Chaim, "I have no idea who he is, but I couldn't ask, 'Who are you?' in case I should have known him. He would have been offended."

When the Gaon and Tzaddik Rav Yeruchem Levovitz died, Rav Chaim organized a group of *bochurim* to learn *mishnayos* in his memory. When the year of mourning ended, the *bochurim* asked him to continue the *shiur*. Rav Chaim obstinately refused. "This *mishnayos shiur* was established in memory of Rav Yeruchem," he said. "If we continue learning after the year of mourning, it will seem as if we didn't do it in his honor."

Rav Chaim had an elderly relative who lived in an old-age home. The man was a *talmid chochom*, and Rav Chaim was very particular to visit him from time to time and talk with him about Torah subjects. Between visits, Rav Chaim would send him letters. On one occasion, he asked a member of his household to mail one such letter. To his surprise, the person mailing the letter saw that Rav Chaim had written "Rabbi Chaim Shmulevitz" on the back of the envelope. He knew very well that Rav Chaim was careful not to refer to himself by any title and certainly not to write the title "Rabbi" on an envelope. He could not resist asking him why he had changed his normal behavior. "This man is an old *talmid chochom*," Rav Chaim responded, "and in the nursing home where he lives, he probably doesn't receive the attention and respect that is due him. Who knows, perhaps if somebody sees that he is receiving a letter from a rabbi, he will be treated differently."

Another anecdote well describes the insight and careful calculation that controlled all his actions: When a great *talmid chochom*, who was also a *baal mussar*, came to Yerushalayim, where he was not well known, Rav Chaim was careful to attend all his public lectures. Although his hearing impairment was so severe that he could not hear what the man was saying, he would sit through his *shmuessen* from beginning to end and look as if he understood every word. The fact that he was present at all these *shmuessen* drew attention to the *talmid chochom's* great virtues. On one occasion, a member of the man's family came to escort Rav Chaim to a *shmuess*, but Rav Chaim shook his head. "I heard he has received an important position in the city. He doesn't need me to attend his lectures anymore."

*   *   *

And the sons of Binyamin [were]...Mupin and Chupin....
                                              *(*Bereshis 46:21*)*

*Binyamin said: "Yosef did not see my marriage canopy, and I
did not see his."*
                                              *(*Sotah 36b*)*

The synthesis of Rav Chaim's intense emotions and intellectual genius resulted in a refined personality, which was
filled with Torah and *mussar*. Once, he stopped at the entrance
to a shoemaker's shop. Little shoes for toddlers were lined up
in a long row. He became very emotional. In his next *mussar
shmuess,* this simple scene was transformed into a major
mussar concept:

I looked at these little shoes and imagined a child
passing by in the street, looking at these shoes, and
wanting them very much. They are obviously expen-
sive, but a loving mother promises her small child that
soon she will have enough money to buy him the shoes.
The awaited day arrives. The child puts the shoes on
his small feet while his mother stands at his side
watching her child with great joy. One can hardly
imagine her joy. I still remember what a father feels at
such occasions. What does a mother feel? I don't know.
But there is one thing I can do. I can participate in her
joy. *Here* [in this world] we can feel the heart of a loving
mother, *Rabosai; there* [in the World to Come] we cannot
share another's feelings.

It is said concerning Adam HaRishon, "It is not good
for man to be alone." But what was so bad about being
alone? He was in the company of angels. They roasted
meat for him and poured him wine. Why was he
"alone"? Living with angels is called being alone be-

cause angels do not have hearts. When one cannot participate with another person, when one cannot connect with the heart of another person, then, even in Gan Eden, it can be said that it was "not good for man to be *alone.*"

Late one night, Rav Chaim passed by the doorway of a carpenter, who was still hard at work. Rav Chaim became mournful. It is a bitter curse, he thought, "With the sweat of your brow you shall eat bread."

During the Six Day War, the yeshiva and people from all over the neighborhood were jammed together in the yeshiva air-raid shelter. Jordanian artillery sent a hail of shells over Yerushalayim, and the Mir Yeshiva building received several direct hits. In the shelter, cries of *Shema Yisroel* and *Hashem Hu HaElokim* were heard.

What do those who are sitting in the shelter shout? "*Ribono Shel Olam*, we are in Your hands, do something." Do you think this is what saved us? No. What saved us was something else completely. Not far from me sat a woman who lived near the yeshiva. The woman was an *agunah* whose husband had left her twenty years ago. You can imagine how difficult her life was. [The painful tone of his voice allowed his listeners to imagine and feel the bitterness of the life of that anonymous *agunah*. He became quiet and shook his head sadly. Then, he suddenly banged on his *shtender*, and with a voice that shook the hearts of all his listeners, he cried out,] She was a laundry woman! She had to wash the dirty clothing of other people, and she saved us. From where she was sitting, I heard her cry, "*Ribono Shel Olam*, I forgive them all." And believe me, she had what to forgive. When I heard this, I knew we were saved. What was she saying? What do you think, *Rabosai*? She was saying, "*Ribono Shel Olam*, see what I can do. You do something as well." And without doubt, this is what saved us.

When Rav Chaim mentioned the name of someone who was *niftar*, he would pause for a moment before adding the words "of blessed memory." That short pause, and the special tone of voice he used, made it clear to everyone that he understood these words clearly and completely. To him, they weren't just an additional title given to the deceased, but were a concept pregnant with meaning.

He argued that it can be seen from *Chazal* when a far-reaching event occurs, one must analyze all its details and understand the importance of every single one, both the good and the bad.

When Yosef was born, Rochel said, "God has gathered in my humiliation." Rashi comments that Rochel could now blame Yosef for anything that happened in the home. "Who broke the vessel? Yosef!"

This is why she needed a son? Do you really think that Yaacov Avinu cared if she broke a vessel? Was it for this that she came to the point of saying, "Give me children. If not, I will die"? Without doubt, Rochel's joy when Yosef was born cannot be described; nevertheless, even on the occasion of this great event, for which she had prayed so much, she did not lose sight of the smallest detail. She called her son by a name which expressed her joy at the smallest detail—"God has gathered in my humiliation."

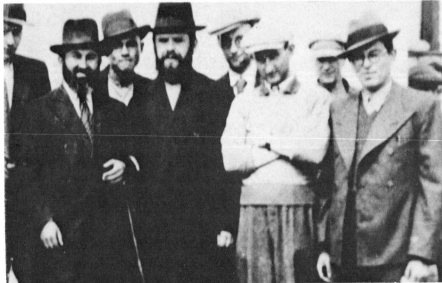

姓名 CHAIM LEJBA SZMUELOWICZ
/IMIĘ I NAZWISKO—/NAME IN FULL/

籍貫誕生 MIEJSCE I DATA URODZENIA SZCZUCZYN. 1908
/PLACE AND DATE OF BIRTH/

職業 ZATRUDNIENIE RABIN - RABBIN
/OCCUPATION/

住址 ADRES 1823A AVENUE JOFFRE
/ADDRESS/

ODCISK P
/THE FINGER

PODPIS
/SIGNATURE/

SZANGHAJ DN. 1 LUTEGO 1943 r.
/SHANGHAI/ W FEBRUARY

PIECZĘĆ

WAŻNA DO
/VALID UNTIL/
1 LUTEGO 194
FEBRUARY

PRZEDŁUŻONA DO
/RENEWED UNTIL/
1 LUTEGO 1945
FEBRUARY

PREZES:
/CHAIRMAN/

SEKRETARZ: Sekretarz
/SECRETARY/   Secretary

Dr. Stan. Tomaszewski.

Inż. M. Krzyżanowski   Inż. M. Krzyżanowski Dr. Stan. Tom

רבינו הכהן לבית לוי

כ"ע פבא אנידרה רב, ורהא שנילוה רא, ורהלרת הנה.
כ"ע רה שנילוה ורהקבין רה, ורבורח שינו רבה אנעה.
תיכתו רבא, ורבכול חולא ס שו שו רקו, ורהלו רל פ.
סעק לא אה נסור, ורהול אל רה רב תלו-רלוננה.
נרית רהב לו הכולם רב רלו, ורלן רה האתנות,
תוס לסיים רב רב רולל, ורהקבלה שלו סקר.

Mareh mekomos for a shiur

When tragic events occur, it is not always the greatness of the tragedy which has to be emphasized. The destruction of the Temple was permeated with suffering, tears, and blood. We find, nevertheless, many sayings of *Chazal* where the prophet specifies minor details or particular personal events that occurred at the time. "It is easier to appreciate the magnitude of the destruction and the exile if we analyze the small details rather than only the general situation."

Rav Chaim argued that were it not for the fact that man has the ability to adapt to most situations and make peace with them, we would never have been able to recover from the Holocaust. The brain can even become used to the Holocaust, he would argue. In order to deepen feelings for the suffering of the Jewish people at that time, he would mention a detail that gave the Holocaust a completely different dimension, one infinitely more terrifying.

Two children were brought to the train which was to carry them to the death camp. Their unfortunate mother stood helplessly by the stairs to the train and begged a German soldier to give her children back. The Nazi said, "You can take one of them." The mother took one of them and crushed him to her breast. The second child fell about her neck weeping and begged her, "Mother, why don't you take me?" She put down the child she was holding and took the second child. The first child burst out crying and said, "Mother, why are you leaving me?" Her heart was torn to pieces. The end of the story was that both young children remained on the train. The unfortunate mother stayed behind. A *gehinnom* like this could not exist even *there*.

*   *   *

Yehudah said to his brothers, "What will we gain if we kill our brother and cover his blood?"
(Bereshis 37:26)

Why did Yehudah merit royalty? [Because he said] "What will we gain if we kill our brother and cover his blood?"
(Tosephta Brochos, chap. 4)

Why was Yehudah different? Surely he sat in judgment with his brothers, and, together with God, they ruled that Yosef deserved capital punishment. But if the situation demanded that they "cover his blood" [so no one would find out what they had done], then they were shaking off responsibility for their actions. This is not judgment—this is murder. This is why Yehudah was chosen as king over them: royalty means accepting responsibility. The Communists shake off responsibility. This isn't royalty. This is murder.
(Rav Chaim Shmulevitz)

As a person who accepted responsibility and had feelings for every Jew, wherever he might be, as a person whose genius in Torah enabled him to comprehend every situation from different perspectives, Rav Chaim was a natural leader to whom everyone turned. The renowned Gaon Rav Aharon Kotler worked hard to persuade him to join the Council of Torah Sages of Agudas Yisroel. In fact, Rav Chaim never took part in any meetings of the Council of Torah Sages, as his deafness made it impossible for him to hear what was being said. Nevertheless, the fact that he didn't appear at official meetings did not put him in the shadows. His stature as a leader whose opinion was sought by all was undeniable.

He firmly refused to become involved in community affairs. Although he was usually the first to be asked to sign important public announcements, he always conditioned his signature on the fact that other *gedolei Yisroel*, whose names he would mention, signed first. "After they sign, come back to me," he would say. When a public announcement was brought to him, he would examine the signatures. If the organizers did not use their own names, or identified themselves in any misleading manner, he would refuse to read the notice: "If he is ashamed to sign his name, why should I read it?"

Rav Chaim never spent more than a few moments on any communal problem. Time was valuable to him. One famous *rosh yeshiva* relates that he participated in an emergency meeting of *roshei yeshiva* at which a problem concerning the very future of the Torah world was discussed, a meeting which took place in a most serious atmosphere. Only a few seconds had passed after the final decision was made, when Rav Chaim was already sitting with an open *sefer* in his hands, learning with great concentration.

Occasionally, he took part in pre-election gatherings called to strengthen *Agudas Yisroel*. His participation was always the key to their success. People used to run to hear how he would present the issues. With short, pointed phrases, he would explain why he did not support the other political parties. At one of these public gatherings, Rav Chaim presented a clear outline, citing sources for his words, as to when, if at all, a *ben Torah* may take part in election campaigning. When he left the *bimah*, he turned to someone close to him and said, "In the yeshiva, I barely manage to finish one sentence before everyone shouts questions and comments at me. Here, I *paskened* a halacha before thousands of people, and nobody has anything to comment." The day after the election, he met a *talmid* of the yeshiva. "Where were you yesterday?" he asked. "The *rosh yeshiva* said that it is permissible to help in the election campaign," answered the *talmid*. "What?" he demanded. "One also has to *listen* to me?"

Anything concerning communal affairs made Rav Chaim suspicious. When emissaries tried to persuade him to take a stand on certain issues, Rav Chaim would carefully analyze and scrutinize the matter. He would only agree to participate if he was sure of the truth of the matter and that the benefits were certain. Whenever he declared his unwillingness to take part, there was no way to change his mind. He often said, "If something is crooked, you cannot persuade me that it is straight." On other occasions, after emissaries had left, he would turn to his *chavrusa* and say, "I know what they *really* want."

With all his modesty and all his reservations, Rav Chaim was still one of the outstanding leaders of religious Jewry. His familiarity with the details of political and communal issues was amazing. Even people who were deeply involved with communal life stood open-mouthed at his knowledge and understanding of contemporary questions.

One can have perfect *middos* without *mussar*, but one cannot change *middos* without *mussar*.

(Rav Yisroel Salanter)

The study of *mussar* shouts, "Change!" *(Mussar shreit, gevald, beit zich!)*

(Rav Chaim Shmulevitz)

ELEVEN

THE ROSH YESHIVA

T HE DEATH of Rav Chaim's brother-in-law, the Gaon and Tzaddik Rav Chaim Zev Finkel, who was *menahel ruchani* of the Mir, left the yeshiva without a *mashgiach*. A few months earlier, the *rosh yeshiva*, the Gaon Rav Eliezer Yehudah Finkel, had also passed away. After the *rosh yeshiva's* death, Rav Chaim said two *shmuessen* in the yeshiva. Until that time, he had only given *shmuessen* in the *Beis Hamussar* in Yerushalayim, on joyous occasions, or outside of the city.

Rav Chaim was very particular not to say *mussar shmuessen* in Bnei Brak. When he was invited to Bnei Brak to give a *shmuess*, he would speak in Tel Aviv instead. When a delegation came to him and argued that there was no point in troubling the Bnei Brak audience to travel to Tel Aviv, Rav Chaim explained that he would not say *mussar shmuessen* in the city where the Gaon and Tzaddik Rav Yechezkel (Chazkel) Levenstein, the *menahel ruchani* of Ponivez Yeshiva, lived. When Rav Chazkel heard this, he sent Rav Chaim a message,

granting him permission to speak in Bnei Brak. Nevertheless,
Rav Chaim refused to say *shmuessen* in the neighborhood of
the Ponivez Yeshiva.

After the death of his brother-in-law, Rav Chaim started to
say regular *shmuessen* in the Mir. Few had heard his *shmuessen*
or his *drashos*, and they revealed a previously little-known side
of his personality. Their format was the same as that of his
shiurim: the questions, the internal divisions, the principles,
the proofs, the conclusions, and the summations in the middle.
Like his *shiurim*, every detail was built on an analysis of the
words of *Chazal*, but the end result led in an entirely different
direction—emotion.

Dry talmudic and halachic principles became living, exciting, human material as they were transformed through Rav
Chaim's sensibilities. Every *maamar Chazal* that he uttered
was clear and enlightening and burned like a fire, inciting the
emotions. Through his penetrating analysis and articulation
of underlying principles, seemingly unconnected sayings of
Chazal suddenly became unified.

Undoubtedly, as both the grandson of the Alter of Novaradok and the grandson-in-law of the Alter of Slabodka, Rav
Chaim was well aware of the *mussar* and educational approaches of both schools of thought. On the *yahrzeit* of the
Alter of Novaradok, Rav Chaim would say *shmuessen* which
included exhaustive analyses of typical principles of Novaradok *mussar*—a *mussar* which emphasized the insignificance
of man. In other *shmuessen*, he elaborated on the concept that
the height of spiritual achievement is an appreciation of man's
greatness—*gadlus ha'adam*—a concept typical of Slabodka
mussar. Rav Chaim's own approach to *mussar* was shaped
mostly by Rav Yeruchem. Although Rav Chaim never totally
accepted the schools of thought of Novaradok or Slabodka,
they appeared side by side in his *shmuessen*. He used them

both, one to analyze the negative aspects of man's personality, the other to analyze the positive aspects. He emphasized the necessity for both in the service of God.

Rav Chaim taught that the development of the positive aspects of man's personality is imperative, for in many situations it is impossible to wage war directly against one's negative aspects. He based his teaching on the words of Rabbenu Yonah, in *Shaarei Teshuvah* (*Shaar* 1:11), which differentiate between "one who happened to sin once...his thoughts and senses not having been alerted to shouting down the sea of lust and drying it up," and "one who finds himself firmly fixed on the wrong path—the beginning of this man's repentance is to forsake his evil ways and thoughts....Only after this must he regret his corrupt ways...."

One who finds himself in the first category should intensify his study of *mussar*. In this way, he will uncover the negative tendencies of his character and will be careful not to follow his *yetzer hora*. One who is already addicted to evil, however, will only damage himself further by confronting his *yetzer hora* directly. The more he analyzes and becomes aware of the negative aspects of his personality, the greater the danger that a fondness for sin will actually grow within him. This type of person must concentrate on the positive aspects of his personality, rekindle these positive aspects, and determine to live by them. This is the first stage. Then, to leave his way of life for good, he must also regret his deeds. Only through regret can he achieve total repentance. It is not enough to simply refrain from sinning. He must uproot *(arois reissen)* the urge to sin. The man who is steeped in sin finds it difficult to tear himself away from his pack of sins. If he only involves himself in good deeds, he will throw off his sins...but the urge to sin will remain.

Yosef revealed to Reuven through his dream that
Reuven's repentance was accepted and that he was
included among the other tribes. The *posuk* then relates
that Reuven returned to the pit. *Chazal* explain that he
returned to his fasting and to his sackcloth. Why?
Hadn't Yosef revealed to him that he was a "shining
star"? The answer is, Reuven went back to his sackcloth
and his fasting to remove the *urge* to sin.

Rav Chaim's *shmuessen* penetrated the hearts and souls of
his listeners. He would use the sharp probe of his *mussar* to
uncover hidden inconsistencies, describing the confused, pa-
thetic man, thrashing about aimlessly, held captive by his own
deficiencies. Although he spoke of the human personality in
very critical terms, when it seemed to him that his words were
too sharp, and they might depress his listeners, he went out of
his way to raise their morale: "I am not speaking to this
audience. You are all *b'nei Torah*. You are all *talmidei chachomim*. I am not speaking to this audience. I am the one who
is ignorant. I am speaking to myself." Rav Chaim would bang
on his heart with his hand. "I know what's going on inside
me."

Rav Chaim never left the audience in a depressed mood,
even after his most penetrating *shmuessen*—on responsibility,
human relationships, egoism, *bitul Torah*, *derech eretz* and the
confusion between light and darkness that exists within the
human personality. His *shmuessen*, even those that were pain-
fully cutting, always contained an element of optimism that
would inspire his listeners. When he approached the end of a
shmuess, reaching his sharpest, most painful point, he would
shake his head and pause briefly, allowing his words time to
leave their impression. Then, suddenly, as if awakening, he
would begin a completely new theme, softly, inspiringly,

optimistically: "*Nu,* what advice should we take? How can a person overcome the situation that he is in? What does a person do in such a situation?"

His *shmuessen* were not composed of abstract ideas. He established principle after principle to concretize physical or spiritual phenomena. These would concern the internal workings of man or creation in general. One or more of these principles were hidden in every *maamar Chazal.* Every explanation contained a surprise; usually the explanation itself was surprising, but very often, the principles themselves were the greatest surprise.

A classic example of Rav Chaim's *mussar* analyses of *maamarei Chazal* draws from the gemara in *Chullin* 110a, which relates how Rami bar Dekula of Pumpedisa was once in Sura on *erev* Yom Kippur. When the townspeople threw away the udders of animals they had slaughtered for the *erev* Yom Kippur feast, he collected them and ate them, in spite of the fact that there was a custom in Sura not to eat the udders of animals (due to the similarity to eating milk and meat together). Rami bar Dekula was brought before Rav Chisda, who asked him many questions about how, why, and when he cooked and ate the udders. In the course of the discussion with Rav Chisda, it also became known that Rami bar Dekula suffered from a stomach ailment.

Rav Chaim spent a long time explaining every single detail of the story. When he finished, the audience still could not work out the connection between the gemara that he was quoting and the rest of the *shmuess.* Finally, after a short pause, Rav Chaim continued:

I am troubled by a very difficult question. Rav Chisda asked Rami bar Dekula many questions, but one question he did not ask him: A Jew is suffering from a

stomach ailment on *erev* Yom Kippur. Why is he search-
ing for discarded animal udders in garbage cans? In
every Jewish home, people are sitting around the table
eating the festive meal of *erev* Yom Kippur. Why didn't
Rami bar Dekula knock on somebody's door? It seems
that one does not ask such a question, for Rav Chisda
understood very clearly the meaning of the phrase, "Do
not ask favors from other people."

Another classic example of Rav Chaim's *mussar* analyses
is found in the following words:

"And it happened one day that Elisha went as far as
Shunam, where there was a great woman. And she
persuaded him to eat a meal. And it was that whenever
he would pass through, he would stop there to eat a
meal. And she said to her husband, 'Behold now I
perceive that he is a holy man of God who passes by us
regularly'" [*Melochim* 2 4:8-9].
    Chazal [*Brochos* 10b] ask: "How did she know that
he was a 'holy man of God'?" One opinion maintains
that she realized he was a holy man of God from the
fact that no flies flew over the table when he ate. The
posuk says that she was a "great woman," meaning,
according to Rashi, "an important woman." The Targum renders, "a sinless woman." Concerning such a
woman, *Chazal* ask, "How did she know that he was a
'holy man of God'?" I ask, *Rabosai*, how did the flies
know? *Chazal* do not ask this question. See what
Chazal knew: it was obvious to them that man does
not necessarily know what flies know.

Rav Chaim was able to expose all the strengths and
weaknesses of humanity, and urge people to look at themselves

critically. But such a critical perspective was only to be applied to one's relationship with oneself. When relating to one's fellow man, said Rav Chaim, a person must have extreme patience and understanding of his friend's weaknesses. He must fulfill the wishes and desires of others even if they are not always entirely correct. "To show honor and respect to another person, even imaginary honor, is an obligation. To take honor for oneself is prohibited."

Rav Chaim arrived at a novel approach to human relationships. Concerning *mitzvos bein odom l'chavero*, he maintained that man is not *punished* for wrong behavior, but that the act itself brings on serious consequences.

Chazal say that Peninah angered Chanah, causing her suffering and pain, in order to inspire Chanah to pray for children, so that God would answer her prayers and bless her with offspring. Peninah, say *Chazal*, acted with a pure motivation. What was the result of her actions? Chanah, the barren woman, gave birth to seven children. But Peninah, who had many children of her own, was punished; her children died. Similarly, the Gemara [*Kesuvos* 62b] relates that Rav Rachumi returned home late one *erev* Yom Kippur to find his wife upset that he was late. As a result, he fell off a roof and died. Is that what she wanted? On the contrary, she wanted him to come home earlier. She wanted to spend more time with him. So why should his punishment be death? Now he won't come home at all!

The answer, both in the case of Peninah and in the case of Rav Rachumi, is that when one causes another person pain, the result is not a punishment—it is a natural phenomenon. Human relationships are like fire. When one puts his hand in a fire, the fire burns. It makes no difference whether it is done with good intentions or without any intention. If somebody is upset—the fire burns.

See how far-reaching this concept is! Resh Lakish [*Niddah* 16b] applied the *posuk*, "He that despises his way shall die" [*Mishlei* 18:16], to one who has marital relations in the daytime. Is it possible that a man incurs the death penalty for breaking the bounds of modesty? See how Abaye explains the prohibition: "He might observe something repulsive in her, and she may become loathsome in his eyes." On the chance that "he might observe" and hurt another person's feelings, the fire burns!

Rav Chaim proved from *Chazal* that certain types of behavior are considered so degenerate that a person who does them may simply forfeit his right to exist. For instance, the death penalty for lack of *derech eretz* is not a punishment, but a loss of the right to live. Rabbi Eliezer (*Eruvin* 63a) comments about a student who decides a halachic question in the presence of his teacher, "I wonder if he will live out his days?" In his will (*Pesachim* 112b), Rebbe commanded his children not to enter their homes suddenly or without warning. This he derived from the fact that the bells on the *kohen godol's* robe gave advance warning of his approach.

I understand that the *kohen godol's* arrival in the holy place had to be announced, but the *posuk* states that the purpose of these bells was also to announce his exit. Does one need permission to leave? And why does the *posuk* say that he wore them "so he would not die"?

This can be understood from the Midrash [*Shir HaShirim* 4:62] which explains that although God had commanded Moshe Rabbenu to take the Jewish people out of Egypt, Moshe still asked his father-in-law Yisro's permission to leave Midian.

The same idea is found in connection with Chananya, Mishael, and Azarya. After being thrown into the furnace, they did not leave until they received permission [*Midrash Tanchuma, Noach*, chap. 10]. Waiting for permission to leave is, at best, a sign of courtesy. Where does it say in the Torah that the rule "Be killed rather than transgress" applies to courtesy? After all, when a miracle saved them from being instantly burned to death, shouldn't they have rushed out of the furnace? We see here the importance of *derech eretz*. The miracle continued. The furnace did not burn them to death before they had permission to leave. This indicates that Heaven agreed with the principle.

"If there is no Torah, there is no *derech eretz*." Without Torah, one cannot understand the true meaning of *derech eretz*, and without *derech eretz*, there can be no Torah. A selfish person who takes everything for himself loses his right to exist.

According to Rav Chaim, God's characteristic of meting out "measure for measure" has nothing to do with punishment. The same principle applies to reward. "Measure for measure," said Rav Chaim, simply means that a person is shown his actions: if he has failed, he is shown he has failed, and if he has succeeded, he is shown that he has acted correctly.

The Torah states [*Bereshis* 32:2]: "Yosef brought bad reports about [his brothers] to his father." Rashi comments that Yosef told his father that his brothers were eating limbs from living animals, treating the children of the maidservants with disrespect by calling them slaves, and were suspected of immoral activities. Rashi adds that Yosef received retribution for all three reports: For reporting that his brothers ate limbs from living animals, they slaughtered a goat and ate its meat after they sold him. For calling his brothers slaves, Yosef was sold as a slave. For reporting his suspicion of immoral activities, Yosef's master's wife attempted to seduce him.

I will tell you the truth. I understand two of the punishments Yosef received—that he was sold as a slave and that he was tested when his master's wife tried to seduce him. But I do not understand how he was punished for the report that his brothers were eating the limbs of living animals. The problem is compounded when we read the Midrash:

"Hakadosh Boruch Hu said to him, 'You say they eat the limbs of living animals. But even when they descend spiritually, they still will not eat without *shechita.*'" Where is the punishment? What difference did it make to Yosef whether they ate the goat with *shechita* or without *shechita?* And what difference did it make to Yosef that they slaughtered the goat at the time of their spiritual descent?

The answer is that "measure for measure" is not a punishment. "Measure for measure" is an attribute of God in which He evaluates a person's actions and shows him his mistake. "See, Yosef?" says *Hakadosh Boruch Hu.* "Even when they have descended spiritually, when the *satan* creates turmoil and they can't think properly, they still slaughter the animal before eating it and do not eat the limb of a living animal."

Do you think it is easy for a man to see his mistake? See what the Torah says. For many years, Yitzchak loved Esav because he enjoyed eating Esav's venison [*Bereshis* 25:28]. Rashi explains that Yitzchak was trapped by Esav's smooth talk. Rivkah, on the other hand, loved Yaacov. How long did this situation continue? Until Yaacov received the blessing, and Esav came in after him. At that moment, Yitzchak was seized with a violent trembling. The Midrash [*Bereshis Rabbah* 67:2] comments that Yitzchak's trembling was greater than the one he had at the time of the *akeidah* when he was lying on the altar about to be offered as a sacrifice. Now we can begin to grasp the significance of "measure for measure." When a person sees his mistake, it causes a trembling more violent than that caused by his belief that he is going to die. *Chazal* relate that when Yitzchak was lying on the altar, the heavens opened up before him, and he saw the *truth*. When Esav came in, he saw the awesome power of *falsehood*.

The Gemara [*Sotah* 10b] says that Avshalom was proud of his hair so he was hung by his hair. The Gemara continues, "*She'ol* (the abyss) was split asunder beneath him." Avshalom was hung by his hair, and at that moment he saw the depths [*she'ol*] of his mistake. "Measure for measure" is the language in which God speaks to man. It can be compared to prophecy. When man misunderstands it, he turns into a false prophet.

* * *

Two harlots came before Shlomo HaMelech [both claiming to be
the mother of a single child]....And the King said, "Divide the
living child in two and give half to one and half to the other."
                                              (Melochim I, chap. 3)

I understand that the true mother would not allow her son to
be cut up. But I have a very difficult question: how did Shlomo
HaMelech know that the false mother would agree to have the
child cut up? She was accused of being a thief. Why did Shlomo
HaMelech assume that she was also a murderess? See the
wisdom of Shlomo HaMelech. Sin cannot be stopped. It starts
with theft and ends with murder.
                                              (Rav Chaim Shmulevitz)

Rav Chaim explained man's problem is that he does not
appreciate his fall after he has transgressed. *Chazal* (*Sotah* 3a)
state, "A person does not commit a transgression unless a
spirit of folly enters into him." Rav Chaim explains that this
"spirit of folly" is when a person believes that his spiritual
status after his transgression will remain as it was before he
sinned.

Chazal [Bereshis Rabbah 15:68] ask: "What was the tree
from which Adam and Chava ate? Rabbi Yossi maintains that it was a fig tree." How did Rabbi Yossi know
it was a fig tree? Rabbi Yossi said: "This can be
compared to the following parable...." See how *Chazal*
understood the human personality! If a person wants
to know from which tree Adam HaRishon ate, all he has
to do is draw a parable from everyday life!
   "A royal prince sinned with a slave girl. When the
king heard about it, he expelled the prince from the
court." How frightful! A prince must act like a prince.
If he fails, he descends from his *madregah* and no longer
has any place in the court.

Where should he go? Rabbi Yossi continues: "He went knocking on the doors of the female slaves." He needs a roof over his head. What goes through his mind? "I can't argue with my father, but the female slaves...they will treat me like a prince!"

"They would not receive him...." See, *Rabosai!* Before the sin he was a prince—all doors opened for him. After the sin, even the female slaves wouldn't accept him! Such a *yeridah*...such a *yeridah*! He goes from female slave to female slave and pleads: "Please let me in, I have nowhere to stay." But they would not receive him. "Finally," concludes Rabbi Yossi, "the one with whom he sinned opened her door and let him in. In the same way, when Adam ate from the tree and was cast out of Gan Eden, he appealed to all the trees, but they would not receive him. The fig tree, from whose fruit he had eaten, opened her doors and accepted him, as it says, 'And they sewed the fig leaves together....' " See what Rabbi Yossi knew. If the fig tree allowed them to take its leaves, one *must* say that they had eaten from that tree!

Let me explain this insight to you. The prince sins and everyone sees his fall, even the female slaves. Who doesn't see it? "The female slave with whom he sinned." She still considers him a prince. She doesn't feel that she caused him to fall, and he doesn't feel that he has fallen. Listen well, *Rabosai.* I say that man is his own female slave. He transgresses and does not feel that he has fallen.

Chazal relate [*Yerushalmi, Brochos* 3:5] how the watchman of a vineyard wanted to commit adultery with a married woman. Before they sinned, they went looking for a *mikvah* so that he would be able to immerse afterwards in accordance with the enactment of *tevilas Ezra* [that a person who has had sexual relations must immerse before studying Torah]. By the time they found the *mikvah*, people had started passing by, and they did not transgress.

A person should tremble with fear when hearing such a story. A man goes to sin in a carefully planned manner. Until he knows how he can purify himself, he will not transgress. And which transgression? A most serious one—adultery with a married woman. *Tevilas Ezra, Rabosai*, was enacted in order to enable a person to study Torah in purity. See what kind of person we're talking about. He's at the lowest spiritual level, ready to commit adultery with a married woman. At the same time, he is at the highest spiritual level, desiring to study Torah in purity. I would like to add one additional point. He looked for a *mikvah before* transgressing. If he would not have been able to learn Torah in purity after the transgression, he would not have transgressed.

This is exactly what we have been saying. A person goes to commit the most serious transgression, but he is convinced that after committing the transgression, he will remain at the same spiritual level. He is the slave girl of his own personality. He transgresses, and he doesn't believe that he has descended in his spiritual level. This is the "spirit of folly" of the human personality.

There was a time, say *Chazal*, when they wanted to cancel *tevilas Ezra*. Rabbi Yehoshua ben Levi said: "Something which protects Jews from doing *aveiros* must not be cancelled." Here, *Rabosai*, lies the salvation. *Chazal* knew how to protect Israel. Man needs protective fences. Through the study of *mussar,* a man can

become aware of his own personality and realize that
he can create these fences for himself.

Rav Chaim declared that the best shield against sin is to
gain an appreciation of man's greatness. He would bring
countless proofs that recognizing one's greatness prevents a
person from transgressing and keeps him far away from sin.

The Gemara [*Shabbos* 12b] rules: "One may not read by
the light of an oil lamp. Rava said, 'If he is an important
person, it is permitted.' An objection was raised: 'One
may not read by the light of the lamp lest he tilt it. Rabbi
Yishmael ben Elisha said: "I will read and will not tilt."
Once he read and almost tilted the lamp. "How great
are the words of the Sages who said that one must not
read by the light of the lamp," he exclaimed. Rav Nasan
said that Rabbi Yishmael actually tilted the lamp and
wrote in his notebook, "I, Yishmael ben Elisha, read
and tilted the lamp on Shabbos. When the Temple is
rebuilt, I will bring a fat sin offering." [This proves that
the prohibition should apply even to an important
person.]' [The answer is that] Rabbi Yishmael ben
Elisha was different because he treated himself as an
ordinary person in respect to religious matters."
    It is prohibited to read by the light of the lamp lest
he tilt it. And what about a person who has *yiras
shomayim*? The law applies to everyone—even to people
with great *yiras shomayim*. Just look at Rabbi Yishmael
ben Elisha—he read and tilted. But for an important
person [who would not tilt even during the week], it is
permitted. See how strong is the emotion of honor. A
feeling of importance is stronger than *yiras shomayim*.

Rav Chaim explained that man is uncomfortable with a drop in his *madregah*. Yosef HaTzaddik argues with the wife of Potifera: if he were to sin, he would lose his powers of prophecy and his position among the tribes.

Rav Chaim was amazed:

Is this how one speaks to an accursed woman? She is at the lowest spiritual level, and he speaks to her about being a prophet? Yes, *Rabosai*, this is how a person speaks. He told her, "I can't lower myself." This is a feeling that even an decadent woman can understand.

Rav Chaim often expounded on the true greatness of the Jewish people.

Chazal state [*Midrash Rabbah, Vayikra* 15:2] concerning the mitzvah to build the *menorah* in the *Mishkan* that God does not need man-made light, for if He did, He would have commanded that the windows be built wider on the outside and narrower on the inside to allow the light to enter. *Chazal* conclude that the purpose of the *menorah* was that the Jewish people should rise in the estimation of the nations, who would say, "See how Israel gives light to Him Who gives light to the world." To us, it is obvious that God does not need our light. But see how *Chazal* understood the greatness of *Klal Yisroel*. *Chazal* had to *prove* that *Hakadosh Boruch Hu* does not need our light. See what *Chazal* conclude: If the reaction of the nations is that "Israel gives light to Him who gives light to world," then it is clear that, from a certain perspective, Israel *does* give light to God.

There is a related story which shows the crucial importance Rav Chaim ascribed to the concept of man's greatness.

The Gaon and Tzaddik Rav Yitzchak Isaac Sher, Rav Chaim's wife's uncle, was referred to as "Uncle Rav Isaac." Rav Chaim once traveled with his nephew to visit Uncle Rav Isaac in Bnei Brak and spent an entire day with him, discussing various *mussar* topics. On the way back to Yerushalayim, Rav Chaim seemed agitated. Suddenly, he turned to his nephew and exclaimed, "Listen to what the rebbe said: *Lemaan yezamercha kavod*. The soul is called *kavod*, as in the *posuk*, '*Ura, kevodi'*— awaken, my *kavod*, meaning the soul. *Lemaan yezamercha kavod* means, 'so that my soul might sing to You.'"

A few months later, in his *hesped* for Rav Yitzchak Isaac Sher in the Slabodka Yeshiva in Bnei Brak, he again referred to him as "rebbe." In another *hesped*, given in the Mir Yeshiva in Yerushalayim, Rav Chaim cited a *maamar Chazal* and said, "How would the rebbe have explained this *maamar chazal*?"

*   *   *

In short, the desire for honor is more impelling than all other longings and desires. Were it not for this lust, a man would eat anything and wear whatever would cover his nakedness.
(Mesilas Yesharim, *chap. 11*)

This is a great chiddush. *We think that eating is just another lust. The* Mesilas Yesharim *teaches us that it is a striving for honor....On the table there are plates, and on the plates there are portions. One person stretches out his hand and takes the nicest portion. We think he is simply a lustful person. See how the* Mesilas Yesharim *understands this act.* "If I am not honored with this portion, somebody else will be."
(Rav Chaim Shmulevitz)

Rav Chaim's thoughts derived from his own experience. He chose the subjects of his *shmuessen* only after he had personally experienced, either physically or emotionally, their significance. It was clear to his *talmidim* that the contents of his *shmuessen* were also hints and chastisements he wanted to deliver to himself. In general, his *shmuessen* flowed directly from his thoughts and experiences of the previous week.

One hot summer day, Rav Chaim stood amid the tumult of the old Central Bus Station in Yerushalayim. The heat was heavy, and the smoke from the buses and the dust they were kicking up burned the eyes and made breathing difficult. All of a sudden, a cold, refreshing wind blew through the station. Rav Chaim sighed and said, "For me the world was created." When he got into the bus, he suddenly came to the realization that the complex transportation system was, in fact, there to serve him. Once again, he exclaimed, "For me the world was created." In that week's *shmuess*, he stood on the *bimah* and revealed his emotions and thoughts. "What makes you say 'For *me* the world was created'? You *rasha!* What do you care if somebody else also benefits?"

Rav Chaim once received a large sum of money from a charity foundation for his personal use. Without delay, he apportioned it among the members of his family. None of the arguments that the money was meant for his personal use had any effect. "*Boruch Hashem,* I have, and *Boruch Hashem,* I can give," said Rav Chaim. Five days later, he ascended the *bimah* and, in a spectacular, inspiring *shmuess,* described to the audience the essence of humanity: man's basic desire is to give and then give some more. He cited the introduction to the *Kuntres Hasfekos,* which states that even if man could go up to the heavens and see the heavenly hosts, he would not enjoy it if he could not return to earth and share his experiences with his friends. "How happy is the man who can give. How happy is the man who has something to give," Rav Chaim continually repeated in the course of the *shmuess.*

One day he was watching the garbage collectors collecting the garbage in their truck. Suddenly, one of them walked up to Rav Chaim, who was deep in thought, and said apologetically, "Rebbe, you might think that I am the one who always goes around collecting the garbage, while my friend sits in the truck and pulls the garbage in. But in another half an hour, you will see that I'm going to be sitting in the truck, and he will be the one down here." Surprised, Rav Chaim stood and thought for a long time, while watching the garbage collectors continue their work. In that week's *shmuess,* he spoke about honor. He explained how everybody views himself as being unique in his profession. He brought many proofs that one must bear this in mind when dealing with other people. One must identify with the person's feelings and be on guard not to hurt him in any way.

In his *hesped* on Rav Chaim, one of the great *baalei mussar* of our generation explained that the few moments of silence with which Rav Chaim began every *shmuess* were not intended merely to create an atmosphere. In those few moments, Rav Chaim searched his heart to see if he was worthy of speaking about the subject he was about to begin. His *shmuessen* reflected sincere and honest soul-searching. How often would he exclaim, "I do not need any proofs. I *know* what's going on *here,"* and bang on his heart with his hand. He once related how he had stood on the *bimah* before one of his *shmuessen* and looked out the window where hundreds of people were being ushered in to hear his words:

I stood on the *bimah*, and I looked at what was going on outside. I saw the crowds trying to push their way into the hall. Some people stood in front of the windows and blocked my view. Do you know what I was thinking

while I was standing on the *bimah* watching them? I
was saying to myself, "You *rasha*. Do you feel the same
way when people leave your *shiur?*"

Using delicate and sublime concepts, Rav Chaim managed
to raise his audience to the level of recognizing the great
significance of minor acts and character traits. He once gave
a frightening example of this when he spoke about the
commentary of the Rambam on the mishnah (*Avos* 4:4): "Rabbi
Levitas of Yavneh said, 'Be exceedingly humble in spirit.' " The
Rambam relates the story of a pious man who, when traveling
on a ship, had his honor degraded by an uncouth person who
urinated on him:

Do you think that one has to perform such an extreme
act in order to trample the honor of another person?
When I am learning *mussar* in the *beis hamedrash*, and
bochurim stand near me involved in everyday conversation—isn't that the same thing?

Toward the end of his life, when he was weak and ill, Rav Chaim was sitting and talking to a visiting *talmid*. "My strength is slowly ebbing away. Do you think this is old age? No, it's not. I have had many strengths. All of them, all that I had, I gave away for Torah."

TWELVE

THE LIVING *SEFER TORAH*

R AV CHAIM "Stutchiner" was not endowed with over-whelming natural talents. Former residents of Stutchin definitely recall that as a child he was not known to have had a phenomenal memory. He acquired his memory through tireless toil, endless patience, and a love of Torah that could not be satisfied. Those *talmidei chachomim* who accompanied Rav Chaim throughout his life often commented that those *middos* which he acquired with immense difficulty eventually became the aspects of his personality in which he excelled. Rav Chaim's life will remain, for generations, an amazing example of the heights of Torah and *mussar* which a person can reach through exhausting toil, and with the power and in the merit of love of Torah. No matter at what stage in his life people knew him, they always said that he personified the concept that Torah exhausts a person's strength.

He was not a *masmid* in the usual sense of the word. A *masmid* is one who devotes every free moment of his time to the study of Torah. Rav Chaim personified the opposite idea: he had to steal spare moments from Torah to tend to everyday matters. Walking, eating, or sleeping, he was completely Torah, and it was Torah that completely filled his thoughts.

In his last days, while lying in a coma, he suddenly screamed, "There is no Torah like the Torah of Moshe!" Someone standing next to his bed heard him say, "The Rashash is incorrect." "Where?" asked the listener. "In *Bava Kama* and in *Gittin*," he answered. "And what about in other places?" the listener asked. Unconscious, Rav Chaim smiled the smile of exalted joy of Torah, which even his great pain and suffering could not stifle.

At his funeral, a hundred thousand people demonstrated their feelings of bereavement and loss. One of the *gedolei Yisroel* eulogized him with the following words:

"The Angel of Death could not overcome him. First he had to exhaust Rav Chaim's strength with deep suffering so he would cease to think in learning. Only then was the Angel of Death able to overcome him and take control of his *neshamah*."

*　　　　*　　　　*

Many waters cannot quench love. Neither can the floods˙drown it. If a man were to offer all the treasures of his house for love, they would be utterly scorned.

(Shir HaShirim 8:7)

When Rav Yochanan was laid to rest, his generation said of him, "If a man were to offer all the treasures of his house for the love which Rav Yochanan had for Torah, he would be utterly scorned."

(Midrash Shir HaShirim 8:3)

When Rav Chaim "Stutchiner" passed away from this world, the feeling of mourning that was shared by all could be similarly expressed: "If a man were to offer all the treasures of his house for the love that Rav Chaim bore for the Torah, he would be utterly scorned."